Your Dog's Best Friend
The Dog Sitter

by

Mary Wattle

DORRANCE PUBLISHING CO., INC.
PITTSBURGH, PENNSYLVANIA 15222

Dorrance Publishing Co., Inc.
701 Smithfield Street
Pittsburgh, PA 15222
Visit our website at *www.dorrancebookstore.com*

ISBN: 978-1-4349-1283-1
eISBN: 978-1-4349-7025-1

Your Dog's Best Friend
The Dog Sitter

In Memory of
Chelsea Girl

Dedicated to all those individuals who take such loving care of their beloved pets.

Contents

Introduction

After ten years of running a dental office, it was time for a change. I just didn't know where to begin. One of my mom's favorite sayings "When someone closes a door, God always leaves a window wide open." I didn't realize how many times this saying would come to play in my life.

One morning, I was having coffee watching a morning show, and they had a guest that brought all these cute little animals. As I sat there watching with enthusiasm, it hit me. I called my mom and I said, "Mom, what do I love more than life?" She said without hesitation: "Dogs."

That morning, I put together my resume and drove down to the local veterinary hospital. As luck would have it, they were looking for a receptionist and I was immediately interviewed by the doctor on duty. Remember, God leaves a window open, and believe me, I jumped right through this window with eyes wide open. I was then called that evening telling me I had the job. I was to start in one week.

Every day was a different experience. You could only imagine the great times, the puppies, the very large to the very tiniest of animals all coming through the front door. Along with the great times, there were some not-so-good times: the very, very sick, young and old; the animals that had been hit by cars; or those that had a hunting accident. You name it, I have seen it all. I'm not sure how these doctors deal with this. I always thought you would have to put your heart on hold when working on these animals. Then I realized they do it because they love the animals.

There were animals that I was close to and felt connections with, and there were others that just came and went. The easiest part of my job was kissing the little puppies and kittens. Every day, I would look at the schedule and anxiously await the animals I was closest to, the ones that jumped on the desk to check in. We had a door that if pushed, it would swing open; Daisy, a mixed breed, knew this every time she came in. She wasn't tall enough to jump on the counter, so she would push the door open and come behind the desk to check in and get her hugs and kisses, as many of the dogs did. I loved talking to the dogs. Their ears would perk up and they knew I was talking just to them. They would tilt their heads to the side in anticipation of the next words to come. The owners would just laugh.

I didn't really help in the back unless needed, but my favorite time was when an animal was having a difficult pregnancy and we all chipped in when the doctors had to perform a C-section. As the puppies were handed to us, we would hold the little one in our hands and rub it hard until it started to whine and cry. When I first saw this, I asked why we had to be so rough and the techs would say, "We want to make them good and mad so they will take air in and breathe." Mother and babies always did great with this procedure. I actually think they were relieved when they didn't have to push anymore to get the babies out. It was easier on mommies and mommies' owner as well. Ah, the good times.

Unfortunately, it was a hospital, and I had seen my share of sadness; the sick that never recovered; the animal whose owners had to make that terrible decision that it was time to say good-bye. This part of the job was the hardest. It hit me hard when I'd lose one of our animals and I was supposed to hold it together. I'd try and be strong, but it killed me inside. My job was to cash people out and take care of all the paper work. I would be doing just that and the tears would just start to stream down my face, uncontrollably. Believe me when I say that I had several clients that would hug me and tell me it was going to be okay. Then my day would continue with the next client, but my thoughts would always be with the one we lost.

In this business, you took the good with the bad. The good was having thirteen Golden Retriever puppies come in for their first shots and wanting one really bad, or the three Yorkie puppies that we did a C-section on and knowing you helped bring them into the world, and they were happy and healthy. This was a job that was hard on my heart, and after four years, I knew it was time for a change.

I had probably about thirty clients that I felt exceptionally close to. A month before I left, I wrote letters explaining my decision to leave. I received notes and gifts and flowers all month long. I truly felt that I did a great job and felt appreciated by these clients.

One client in particular that brought their Golden Retrievers in all the time were Paul and Lane. She was sorry to see me go and she wrote me a nice card. She actually came up on my last day and I was so sad to see her; I just didn't want to say goodbye. I happened to mention that if they ever needed me to watch the dogs instead of bringing them in for boarding, I would be happy to and she could call me anytime. I didn't say this to take business from the hospital, but it was because I couldn't stand when the dogs came in and sat in kennels day after day while their owners were on vacation. I thought to myself, there had to be a better way. This is where my story begins and my new window opens up.

Bright Eyes and PT

(Bright Eyes and PT playing near the driveway)

Lane called me about two weeks after I left the hospital. She asked if I was serious about watching their dogs while they were gone. I said, absolutely. Was I okay with staying at their home while I do this? I told her it was exactly why I would do this: The owners go on vacation and the pets are safe and happy at home. The day came when I was to meet with Lane and she would show me around and what was what. I drove down this very long driveway and was met by two beautiful Golden Retrievers, Bright Eyes and PT. I hadn't realized how much I had missed these two dogs. So down the driveway they chased me not knowing who was in the car, they jumped and barked while their tails were wagging. Oh no attack dogs, I said to myself.

I stepped out of the car and the look on their faces said it all. "Oh, my gosh, Bright. It's that girl from the hospital." "It's Mary! Hi-hi-hi." I thought they were talking to each other like that. Excited and jumping all over me, I was greeted with love. Lane showed me around the house and then we went for a walk around the property so that I knew where they walked. I was told they go for these walks three times a day if not more. That would be up to me. They ran, walked, played with each other the whole way around. As I came into the house, I realized the dogs have all the say here, and just let Paul and Lane live there with them. I said to myself, "I like it." Such love these two people have for their pets.

I was a little nervous my first night. I had never done this before and now I was in charge of the house and their beloved pets. Their backyard was Lake Erie. I knew there were 121 steps down to the beach, and thought to myself, what if they get to close to the edge or go down to the beach without me, will they run away? I eventually learned that they knew exactly where the cliff was and they rarely strayed from the house. On our first night, PT was on the couch right next to the chair so he could be easily petted for hours at a time, and if at anytime I stopped petting, his paw would automatically come up and scratch my arm to continue. Bright's spot was right in front of the chair so my left hand was free to pet her, while my right hand was petting her brother. I soon figured out that PT was an alpha dog. He ran the show. If he heard a sound, he would jump off the couch, barking and carrying on until I let him outside. Bright would follow suit.

(PT, Mary and Bright Eyes getting petted 24/7)

On our walks, she followed him everywhere. He was the leader. He ate first and he had his spot on the couch. Believe it or not, Bright was fine with this. He was more intense than her, while she was way more laid back. I thought it funny; they were just like kids with the same parents but two different personalities. On our first night, and I didn't know what to expect. Lane had big comfy beds for them with their names on them and they were strategically placed in the bedroom. I said, "Come on, it's time for bed." They got right up and went into the bedroom and lay on their beds. I turned out the lights and hopped into the king-size bed that I would be sleeping in. Then two seconds later, they jumped in bed with me and we were having a slumber party. That was the first night I realized that I would be sleeping with two 75 pound goldens, and I was in the middle. This way the petting could continue even in bed.

They live in a pretty big house and it is very secluded and dark, but I felt very comfortable being surrounded by protection. I also became very aware, in the middle of the night, that sleeping with two very large dogs was like sleeping on the middle rack of an oven. I woke up sweating and stripping off my pj's. In the process of trying to cool down, I realized I woke them and the petting had to begin again. It was like waking a crying baby; if you rock them, they slip back to sleep, and soon again they were snoring, and everyone fell back to sleep. I chuckled to myself and said this was the greatest job ever.

Morning came and I heard a bark at the front door. Not sure who was out there visiting at this time, but PT and Bright seemed to know just what was going on and I was clueless. So I scrambled to see what they were barking at and it was Chip, the Beagle.. He was at the door barking to get in. I knew that Chip lived up the driveway with Lane's daughter Nancy and her husband Steve. I thought it was awfully early for a visit, but apparently this was an everyday occurrence, which I would later find out. They all seemed extremely happy to see one another. Chip spent all day with us, went on our walks, and we all ate together. I figured this was how it usually was. Chip was such a cute Beagle it was perfectly fine with me. Nancy or Steve would come down every night at 8:30 P.M. to get chip and take him home for the night. If you ask me, I think he would prefer to stay for the slumber party, but that was not happening tonight.

(Chip on couch amidst all the pillows)

The longer you're with the dogs, you soon begin to learn their little quirks. They loved their walks, and I soon found out they loved car rides also. Of course, PT was always in the front seat, getting petted the whole time, and believe me if you stop, you get the paw across your arm. He was relentless with this petting. It was like my hand was a pacifier for him. Bright got the whole back seat to herself, where she comfortably laid down. She changed position often. Sometimes, she would be sitting with her head lying on the back seat looking out the back window, and other times she just lay across the whole back seat. She was just content to be in the car.

One time, I had this great idea to drive them down to the peninsula and take them for a walk. I grabbed their leashes and off we went. I won't tell you how much I weigh, but I will tell you they weigh more than me. I got PT out first and put his leash on him, then it was Bright Eyes's turn to get out. They were so excited to be there, so they took off, one went one way and the other went another way, back and forth, twisting my body this way and that way. I had absolutely no control over these dogs. I thought to myself, they were so easy on their property. Just leisurely walking and having fun, but not here. They were so excited they couldn't even see straight.

We went about twenty feet and then I turned them around and came back to the car. I was exhausted. I sat there and just said to myself, "Oh my God, what was up with that. I feel like I just took an hour of aerobics class." Then I realized they never go for walks on the peninsula; they don't have to because they have acres and acres to run on, leash-free, at home. Needless to say, all our walks were going to be at home from now on. We headed home and I felt so

4

guilty for not going for that long walk I promised them that I stopped by the local ice cream parlor and got them baby vanilla cones. All was forgiven.

(Bright Eyes out in the first snow of the year)

In the morning, they go out right away then they come in and eat breakfast. They sit patiently in the kitchen waiting for their bowls to be placed in front of them. They gobble that down as if it's going to be their last meal, and then they fly back outside and wait again for me to get dressed and finally they hear those five little words: "Let's go for a walk." Their ears pop up and they start running and jumping and we're off for our morning walk. Chip most often catches up with us and all is good in the world. During the weekday, I clean houses so it really works with my dog-sitting. I can do our morning routine and go to work, and while I am gone they sleep. I will be gone for three hours then home for lunch and another walk, then back to work for another three hours. Once they know the routine, they know I am coming back, so they sleep to get ready for the night's festivities.

When I started this, I decided to keep a diary of the day's activities, and this way when Lane and Paul get home they can read about what we've done. I didn't realize how this would come into play till much later. Lane calls at night to check on them and make sure everything is okay and she gets the same answer every time she calls. Everything is fine.

One night around two in the morning, the dogs started to bark. If it's a clear night and the moon was out, then it's like daylight at this house. This particular night the dogs started barking like crazy. At first, I was scared because I didn't know what the dogs were barking at, then I looked outside and saw the deer about eight feet from the window eating the berries off the trees and bushes. This time I let the dogs out because they were going nuts. They chased the deer across the field. Like I said, it was so lit from the moon I could see it all. Of course, the deer were a lot faster than the dogs. They came back to the house and it was back to bed, we were all sleeping again within half an hour. After that I never let the dogs out at that time of night, I just let them bark until they got it out of their systems. The deer needed to eat and have their time as well, so I was just being fair. Once you learn the dogs' little quirks, this job becomes easier and easier.

(Me and Bright at Thanksgiving)

Fall turned into winter. It's the dogs' favorite season; they love snow. Bright sits outside the kitchen door for hours just looking out into the front lawn and fields. I check on them because I think they must be cold by now. They are covered in snow from head to toe. They just look up at me as if to say, "What?" They love walking in the snow and I have to say the pine trees are beautiful with snow on the branches. It always looks like a winter wonderland here, so I have to say I love the walks as much as they do. I look over at Bright Eyes and she is on her back making a snow angel. I swear when she stood up, she had a smile on her face. She would then shake off all the snow..

(Bright outside the door just enjoying the snow)

One day runs into the next and they don't care if their owners are home or not. Their day doesn't change at all, so it doesn't bother them that Paul and Lane are gone. They call weekly to check on them, but they are never worried about the dogs while I am here. Their vacations just got that much better, which was my objective from the start, and to spoil the dogs, but that goes without saying.

PT and Bright didn't get groomed regularly, and sometimes they would roll in something that wasn't quite pleasant or they would sometimes go for a dip in the lake, which just meant they would smell like fish. So one by one they went into the tub. They didn't like getting into the tub, but they didn't seem to mind their baths. I would then comb them out and blow them dry. They loved this part. They loved the blow dryer. It was nice and warm and they loved getting brushed. They liked the attention, not to mention they smelled better when I was through.

It's Christmastime and I was back with PT and Bright for another holiday season. This year for Christmas I gave them a new dog stand with bowls. It's up high so they don't have to bend over so much when they eat. They love that but not as much as they love their new toys. PT got a stuffed raccoon, which he absolutely loved, and Bright got a green rubber ball. She loved to have the ball in her mouth all the time. Sometimes, she walks on our walks with it the whole way, only putting it down when sniffing something on the ground.

(Bright Eyes on her big bed with her green Christmas ball)

(PT with his raccoon. I was not getting this back)

Lane always feels bad because I am always away from home for the holidays, so she told me that I could have a New Year's Eve party if I would like. She had put in another stove and cook top in their kitchen, so it was easy to prepare a lot of food at one time. I took her up on her offer to have a party. The weather in this area is always iffy, but because everyone is used to it, people come out despite the snowy weather. It was a great turnout and everyone came. There had to be at least 50 people there. The dogs were just great. They are such people-person dogs. They loved everyone, and vice versa—all my guests just thought the dogs were great. I had Chip, Chipper, Bright and PT.

Chipper is another dog I watch and I brought him to Lane and Paul's for the holidays. Chip and Chipper hung out in the dining room just waiting for food to drop suspiciously to the floor. Whereas, Bright and PT would walk around and in hopes to get people to pet them. My guests would put party hats on them and they would wear them proudly. They were great sports.

It was a fun party, and believe me, the dogs and I were very tired on January 1. We knew we rang in the New Year with a bang.

(Chipper on the side table, his safe zone)

(PT celebrating New Year's Eve with everyone)

At times, when they didn't feel good or they just weren't themselves, I would have to take them to the vet hospital. Lane didn't take any chances with them. They went whenever I felt it was necessary. Bright was great. She just went and jumped on the counter to see who was behind the desk. PT was good until they called his name, then he would just plant himself. I literally had to drag him into the room with one of the techs pushing him from behind.. What a big baby. This is the one time I would say, little dogs are easier, for you can carry them into the examining room.

One time I came over and Lane left me a note that said PT wasn't going for walks. He had somehow touched the electric cow fence, which was about three acres away from the house, and got a shock, so now he wouldn't go past the driveway. So every time we'd go for a walk that week, they would start the walk by running, and then PT would come to a dead stop like he just ran into a brick wall. He wouldn't go any further; he would sit there and patiently wait for us to come down the driveway, then as soon as he'd see us he'd start jumping around and run back to the house, like he'd been on the walk with us. I'd just look at him and say, "Baby, you missed a good walk." After two days of not walking with us, I put the leash on him and made him walk with us. That's all it took. He was fine after that and forgot all about the fence, but he did stay away from it when we walked around the cow pasture. Like I said, funny quirks, live and learn.

(Bright and PT tuckered out from the day's activities)
(Thank God, mom and dad have a really big couch)

Chip

(Chip in the flower bed at Paul and Lane's)

As you have already heard, Chip is a Beagle. This is one of the cutest Beagles I have ever seen. I first met Chip when Nancy brought him up to the hospital for his puppy shots and most of you will agree there is just nothing cuter than a Beagle puppy. I only saw Chip when he would come in to the hospital for his yearly shots.

Nancy and Steve have decided to move into the house that Lane grew up in and it is right down the driveway from Lane and Paul. This means that Chip is no longer in a neighborhood where he had to be on a leash or just in the backyard. He had acres and acres to run on, and best of all, I get to see a whole lot more of Chip than before.

Every day, Chip came to visit. He loved Paul, and I would like to say he loved me as well. When Chip comes down and it's the first time I am seeing him that day, he just sits there and howls, and then I howl back at him and he howls back again. This goes on for at least five minutes then it's business as usual for Chip. This means it's time to sniff the ground and run. For me, it was time to clean. Chip always found his way back in time to go for our walk, even though he had been walking and running the whole day. There was something about going for a walk with the whole gang together, even though he never stayed with us. He starts with us and ends with us. It's just something about saying to them, "Okay who wants to go for a walk?", and Chip is the first one to head on down the driveway towards the fields. I absolutely love this little Beagle.

At times I am watching all three dogs. This is Chip's favorite time when he gets to sleep over. Chip loves to nap on the couch, or Paul's chair, anywhere that's not his own bed. At night he is the first one down the hallway to bed. PT and Bright get on either side of the bed, and that leaves the middle for Chip and I. Chip is at the bottom of the bed. He knows because of his size he is low man on totem pole, so he doesn't mind. At home he sleeps in the kitchen on his doggy bed, but when he gets to sleep over with Bright and PT, he gets to sleep in the bed with us. Life is good.

Morning comes and he eats and he's off. If I have to go to work sometimes, I am forced to leave him outside until I get back from my morning house. Whenever I drive down the driveway at lunchtime, he is often sitting by the tree waiting for me. It is normal for Chip to be off and running all day; every day is an adventure for Chip. But he always comes home for every meal and he is in the house by dark for a good night's sleep because you just don't know what tomorrow will bring. So kisses on his little head and then off he goes. As he goes off, I yell at him, "Be safe, my little friend."

(Chip out in the field on one of his walks)

Christmases were always spent with me. Nancy and Steve were only gone for a week at Christmastime, whereas Lane and Paul were always gone for a month or so. When Nancy and Steve got home from vacation, they came down every night to get Chip at 8:30 P.M. Every morning, he would make his way down to the house to be with Bright and PT, then Nancy would come down to bring him home. Sometimes I would call to see if he could have a sleepover with us and most often Nancy would say yes. I would just hang up the phone and say to Chip, "She said yes. You can stay," and I swear he knew what I had just said to him. His tail would wag and he would settle back in on the couch. It might have been the pitch of my voice or the fact that I just kissed his head, but he always knew when it was going to be a sleepover.

One time in January, Nancy was home and Chip had come down right after breakfast. He went on our walk with us and then off he went. It was cold and I wanted Chip to be in the house before I left, so I had to wait around till he got cold enough to come home. I was calling him because it was getting later and later. I heard him barking and I didn't like where the barking was coming from. So I reluctantly went to the bank. Now, in order for you to get a true picture of what I was seeing, I have already said there are 121 stairs from the top of the bank to the beach below. My fear was confirmed, there he was way out on the ice of Lake Erie, he had his nose to the surface sniffing what I could only imagine were fish.. He was not paying attention to me and my heart was beating faster and faster. I could just see him falling through the ice and disappearing before my eyes. I raced back to the house because he was ignoring me and I needed some help. I called Nancy who drove down to the house and together we tried to get his attention. We got down to the beach with a leash in our hand just hoping we could get his attention before he fell through the ice. Half an hour went by and his nose was glued to the ice still. We discussed going and getting the fire department, but thought the dog was not in the water and how could we take them away from maybe someone that could really use them, not that we couldn't but we were caught between a rock and a hard spot. So we decided against calling. We walked back up the stairs and I just couldn't watch anymore. Nancy said, "There isn't anything we can do without putting ourselves in danger, so let's just hope for the best." We both went to work reluctantly.

(Chip was really out that far on a freezing cold Lake Erie)

It was a long morning for me. I couldn't clean my morning house fast enough. All I could think about was Chip on the ice. As I drove back to the house for lunch, I just prayed that he was sitting by the door waiting for me. As I drove up the driveway, I didn't see him. I got a pit in my stomach, then on the other side of the tree I saw movement. As I drove up he came around the tree and looked at me as if to say, "What?" I kissed his head then I yelled at him. I actually never saw him do that ever again. Now whether he did, I don't know, but I never caught him. You hear stories like this in the news all the time and it always breaks my heart, even though the stories they report usually have a happy ending. I am sure there are a lot of stories we don't hear that end badly. I am just thankful this one was a good ending.

I swear Chip is or was a cat in another life because he has nine lives. He has several aliases as well. One time we were on our walk and his head was stuck in a ground hog's hole. He was halfway in and halfway out. I kept calling him, but again I was ignored. He's stubborn that way. I knew where this was heading, so I just kept walking and hoped for the best. An hour later he was barking at the front door. He walked in like nothing was wrong. I noticed blood on the floor dripping. I checked him all over and now I had blood on me. I couldn't find anything on his body or his face. Then I noticed his ear. A piece of it was missing. When a dog's ear is bleeding, it's like when a guy cuts himself shaving, it's hard to stop the bleeding. So I applied pressure to it, but to no avail. I couldn't get it to stop. So I cut up one of Lane's turtleneck shirts. I flipped his ears over his head and wrapped them with gauze, then I placed the neck of the shirt that I had destroyed around his head and his ears. It held.

I said that would have to do until I could clean it in the morning. Chip was so tired he went to bed and didn't bother his new hat. After that, I started calling him Evander, after Evander Holyfield, if you get my drift. That was just one of the nicknames. Never a dull moment with this little Beagle.

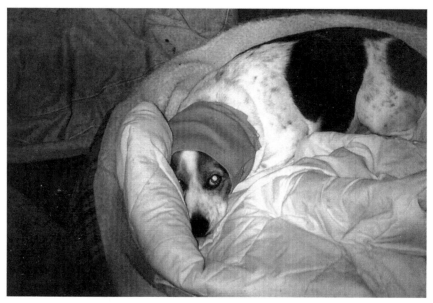

(Chip with his turtleneck bandage on, my ear hurts)

On days when I cleaned Lane's house, which was twice a week, he would sometimes already be down there waiting for me, and other times he would just be sitting outside of his own house. When he was there he would see my car and start to run down the driveway chasing me. I would be parked and standing by my car waiting for him now. As I watched him running toward me, I remember one time David, Nancy's son, call him Batdog because his ears would be flapping in the air while he ran and it looked like he was wearing a cape, so the nickname Batdog would stick as well. The howling would begin and we would have a grand hello and the day would begin with a walk as usual.

Chip would head off into the fields and all you could see was his tail, like Snoopy. It was the cutest thing to see only that tail in the air. I would just say to Bright and PT, "There goes Snoopy." Then he would get on the scent of something and the chase and the howling would begin. Often PT would go and investigate while Bright stayed by my side. Chip would never catch anything, but the chase was always fun.

Chip was loving life here with all this land to run on and all these creatures to chase. He loved having his two best friends, PT and Bright, to run with him. Life was good for this Beagle as it would be for several years to come.

Chipper

(Chipper with Kristyn, Michael, and Alec down at the Peninsula)

I often got new clients by coincidence. I was shopping at our mall and I ran into a friend I hadn't seen in a while, Jo. One thing led to another and before I knew it I was cleaning her house as well. At that time she had a rabbit named Molly, a cat named Sassy, Lucy the cockatoo, and something she fed grasshoppers to, which was the one thing I did stay away from. Needless to say, she loved her animals. One day I came to work and she had a fluffy little puppy they named Chipper. Chipper was a Shih Tzu, and may I say, so stinking cute. I would carry him around in a back pack that I would turn around and have him in front of me on my chest while I cleaned. He was really small.

Jo knew that I watched dogs and had asked me to watch Chipper over Christmas. Unfortunately, I am always at Lane and Paul's for the holidays, so I asked them if they would mind if I brought Chipper over and watched him at their house. Of course they didn't care. Lane would say the more the merrier.

Chipper got in my car and was happy to be there. He loves to go for car rides. When we pulled up to Paul and Lane's, Chipper got out and was checking all the smells in the yard. PT and Bright heard us pull up so they were going a little crazy to see me. I picked up Chipper because he is about seven pounds and PT and Bright Eyes are about seventy-five pounds each, and very curious. I didn't want them to think Chipper was dinner. I have to introduce them slowly to each other. Poor Chipper was extremely scared, but after the curiosity wore off it was business as usual. They knew it was time for their walks, so off we went. Chipper was more than happy to go for a walk. PT and Bright sometimes sniffed Chipper during the walk, but for the most part it was just another dog to them.

At night the dogs took their usual places, Bright at my feet, PT sitting on the couch to my right, and now Chipper sat on the end table on the left-hand side of me. I think he felt safest there. He was off the floor and if he sat up on his hind legs he would be eye to eye with Bright, she wouldn't be so intimidating then.. It was a great Christmas, the dogs got all new toys; Chip got a new bed and they all got treats. I made eggs and bacon on Christmas morning and shared with all the dogs. Now remember, it's Christmas so that means I have Chip as well. So I have Bright and PT, Chip and Chipper. It was a Christmas doggy day care. Some of my favorite memories came from this holiday at Paul and Lane's.

(Chipper sitting on table next to my chair on New Year's Eve)

I clean once a week for Jo, so I get to see all their animals on Tuesdays, plus they almost always go away on vacation at Easter and one week in the summer. They would always leave before I got there, but Chip knew someone would be coming to take care of him. When I pulled into the garage he would just go nuts. He was so excited to see me. He'd follow me all over the house. I would first bring in my luggage and he would follow me upstairs. If I was watching television he was on the couch. He would stop sometimes to chase Sassy down, but immediately came back to my side. He didn't want me to pay any attention to the other animals, so he would chase Sassy off if she got too close.

Chipper had such personality. Jo knew that when they left for vacation they didn't have to worry about leaving the animals. I don't even think they ever called me once when they were gone. That was how much they trusted me with their zoo. Every time I came through the door, Chipper would come running, "She's here, she's here, where's my treat?" Knowing I carried Pupperoni with me. There wasn't anything Chipper loved to do more than eating. Snacks or whatever I was eating at the time would do. He wasn't picky about his food. "Now go put that suitcase away and take me for a walk," so off we'd go down one side of the street then back again. He really didn't need long walks; any size will do.

My favorite time with Chipper was bedtime. He'd chase Sassy, the cat, up the stairs, but then jump in bed and wait for me to get in. He would snuggle right up to me and we would either watch TV or just go right to bed. It didn't matter what we did, as long as we were together in that bed.

During the week, I'd have to work as usual, so we would get up early because we had a lot of animals to feed, and then after Chipper was done eating, we'd go for our walk. In the summer, we would have our breakfast out on the patio, coffee for me and water for Chipper. He'd run around the backyard for a while, then I was off to work. I would leave the TV on for him. He would get on the leather couch and wait, knowing I'd be home for lunch to walk him again.

Finally the weekend would come and Chipper knew it was drive time. That's right, "Come on, Mary, lift me up to my throne." Up and in Chipper would sit on the console. He would be right next to me so he could see where we were going. It didn't matter where we were going, just that we were going—the store, a friend's house, and sometimes to my house, where he would chase my cats—for something different to do. Sometimes he would be so excited he would poop in my dining room. He'd look at me as if to say, "Oops, I got a little excited. I was so excited to be here. I forgot to go to the bathroom before I came in. Sorry." It was no big deal. It was like picking up tootsie rolls. Sorry for being so graphic. Back to the car and on our way home again, "I look over at Mary and just say, 'What?'" I was looking at him like I could not believe he did that in my house, and then I would just laugh. He would have no other choice but to lean into me and lick my face and that took care of everything. All was forgiven.

Chipper has one of those faces that you could see every emotion in his eyes. I pretty much knew what he was thinking at all times through his facial expressions. Easy to read if you pay attention to the different looks he gives you.

Like PT and Bright, I would write a journal to the family so they knew exactly what we did while they were away. Luckily for me, Jo kept these journals. I was told she would read this to the family and they all got a chuckle out of it. So they always looked forward to the journals when they came back home.

Look who's here? Lick, lick, lick. Oh, I am so excited. I followed Mary around all night. Sassy is eating and I am just sitting watching Mary. The week went by so fast I am going to summarize it for you. Every night we sat out on the patio. I say we because Mary let Sassy go out also. We all sat on our own chairs and Mary was reading a book while Sassy and I just looked around. Mary and I would walk every morning and evening. I love my walks, except when a loud car goes by. I have been pooping down on the corner in the border bushes. I just back in and go. Mary picks it up, of course. Well, I don't have thumbs so I can't pick it up myself. I've eaten a little bit of Mary's food. On Saturday, we made two trips to Wal-Mart, and I was very good each time. We shared a vanilla cone. One day, I got to work with Mary. I visited Bright Eyes and PT, and I get along with Chip (the beagle) real well. We went for car rides as often as possible because she said I was such a good rider. Every morning I'd get on the kitchen stool and I get my ear medicine, which I didn't mind. I love my time with Mary. At night when she's watching TV, I will curl up on Mr. Scarecrow's legs, and she tells me I am adorable. Our last night together, she petted me all night long. When we woke up, I was lying right next to her head. She said that called for some cuddling. I don't like to see her go, but, oh I love to have you all home.

Love Chipper, the dog

I was never in my cage when Mary's home. I cried the moment I saw her. I poop anywhere I please. I like to walk on the marble floor and I even get on Mary's sneakers for a ride. I eat a ton of cheerios, and as Mary always says, I'm not the neatest of eaters. Oh yeah, show me a bird that is. Anyways, I annoy Mary every morning by climbing on her and eating her earrings, and chewing on the laces of her sneakers. Then I climb on her chest and she pets me and slowly my eyes close and by 10 P.M. I have fallen asleep and in my cage by 11 P.M. It's a bird's life.

Love Lucy, the bird

Quiet as usual. Meowed to the outside. Stood on the top of the stairs and meowed. Would only let Mary give me my medicine once a day. Slept on the bunk beds all day and night. I stood in front of the screen door and tried to catch the bugs. That's my favorite part of the day. I was my usual good self. Had several treats. It's a lazy cat's life and it's all mine.

Love Sassy, the cat

I stay in my cage 'til Mary gets home, then I get to go to my bigger pen where I run around, dig holes, and stretch out. Hop, hop, hop, life goes on.

Love Molly, the rabbit

When they first brought Chipper home, they had a blanket with a bear's head attached to it. He would lay on top of the blanket and put his paws around the head of the bear's face and just suck on the bear's nose. It was so cute. Just like a baby with its favorite blanket. He loved his bear blanket. I love this dog.

I have found out that Shih Tzus are one of the most loyal dogs to their owners. If I come across owners of a Shih Tzu, they cannot say enough about the love for their dog or dogs. Most often if they have one, they have had them before. That's just how much they love them. They have such great personalities and spunk they make a great family pet. Back to another week with Chipper and friends.

Saturday

I wept for quite a while then I gave up. Then it happened. Mary came. Yeah, she's got a bag that means she is here for the durations. Oh, happy day. We went out and watered the plants. Mary loves that I don't go out of my lawn except to go to the next-door neighbors for a cookie. I got two of them today. We went for a walk, quite enjoyable, then we went for a car ride also, yeah. Burger King, it's dinnertime. I got a biscuit from the lady in the drive thru window and I ate it up in the back window. Then I had some chicken and fries for dinner. I was up on Mary's chest lying down and Lucy was on her leg. I don't care when Mary talks to Lucy or to Sassy. I just don't want anyone to be around her except for me. However, I won't let Sassy around her at all. Lucy fell asleep on her legs and I moved down to my bean bag pillow and hugged my teddy. All is right with the world again. I'll be going for a walk in the morning, so I am going to get some sleep. Goodnight.

Sunday

We slept till 8 am so I know Mary doesn't have to go to work today. We got everybody fed. Well, I didn't really do anything but watch. We sat down and ate cereal, now I did help with that. Lucy was up on her perch in the kitchen, Molly was in her cage outside. Mary took a shower and I waited for her right outside of the shower door. We went for a walk. Did I say I love that? One of our neighbors up the street was playing the opera music a little too loud, it frightened me, but Mary kept walking so did I. We watered the plants, I started crying because I couldn't find her, then I realized I was outside so I ran around the front and there she was. Man, that bird requires a lot of Mary's attention; I'm not liking that so much. We went for a walk at 7:45 and Mary felt like this was a stepford neighborhood. She said people were walking their dogs (including me), kids were playing at the end of the street, and people were riding their bikes. It sort of freaked her out a little. We got home and watched a movie. I lay on the floor with teddy and Lucy fell asleep on her lap. It seems to be a habit with her. We had some granola cereal for a snack and went to bed.

Monday

Oh no, she's setting the alarm, so that means she has to work in the morning. I'll pout and see what that gets me. I know I go for walks and rides in the car, and I get petted whenever I want, but Lucy does take up too much of Mary's time, especially in the morning. Yes, I am complaining. I am used to being the "one." Now I have to share her. Don't like it one bit. Hey, she's home, she's home and it's only noon. Mary is home early and she has brought us lunch. Yeah, the pouting worked. She is home for the afternoon and I got a few bites from her hamburger. We spent the afternoon out on the patio. Mary read and I moved around the chairs. Molly had a ball in her outside cage. We washed Mary's car, well I just sat on the steps and watched her. I was no help until she asked me to vacuum her car out, mostly it was crumbs from me so I was happy to oblige. We had chicken pot pie for dinner and popcorn for snack. I eat everything except my food. Lucy calls over to Mary about 8:30 and sleeps on her chest till about 10 P.M. every night. It's becoming a habit. Anyways, I slept on the bathroom floor because I was hot, until it started to thunder, then I scrambled up to Mary's side and slept through the night.

Tuesday

We got up early and Mary did her routine, which she spends too much time on Lucy as usual, but I did get to go for my morning walk, and then Mary did it. She left. I cry for a while, then Sassy tells me to shut up and I chase her, and she retreats into Michael's bedroom and I have won again. Yeah, she's home. Hi, hi, hi, Yeah, put Molly out. I'll come with you. Sometimes, I miss you guys and I kind of mope around, but then Mary gets dinner and I am better. We sat outside and read and then we went for a walk. Now Lucy is on her perch in the kitchen. Molly's back in the garage, and Sassy's sitting by the screen door, and I am on the coffee table. Another good day.

Wednesday
Mary put on her peach short set, which has the silly buttons on it that Lucy tries to peck off. Mary keeps yelling at her for it; I just shake my head. I had some special time this morning. Mary woke up first to find me fast asleep on the pillow next to her. She started petting me, that was such a nice way to wake up. We laid there for a while then we had to get up and tend to everyone else, much to my chagrin. Mary got home pretty early in the afternoon. She put Molly right out in her big cage and I just stood there and cried, you know that cry that makes you come running because something's wrong. I don't know why, nothing was wrong, I just wanted her to pay attention to me and not to Molly. I am not spoiled. We sat outside and Mary read a little then she watered the plants. I ran next door and watched the rabbits. They have more than one so I sat there and watched them while Mary watered. I got bored watching her so I found my own thing to do. We went for a walk, but I didn't want to go tonight. I kept stopping and looking at her so we came back and she took me for a ride instead, which is what I was going for. We drove and drove and drove, we were going to stop for ice cream then Mary decided not to. Not my choice by the way. So now we are set- tling in for the night. I'll be on my teddy, Lucy will fall asleep on Mary's chest, and then we will go to bed, and that's my special time—me time.

Thursday
Wow, that was a really long day without Mary. It started out pretty much the same way. We woke up, fed all the animals, and cleaned the cages. I watched her blow her hair dry, she puts me right on the counter and talks to me the whole time she is drying. After my walk, Mary left and we didn't think she was ever coming home. It was her long day. We let her have it. When she came through the door, I was barking and wagging my tail and even Sassy was meowing loudly, and you should have heard Lucy squawking. I felt terrible for Mary. She really got it when she came home. Well, she made up for it. She stayed up late and spent time with all of us. It pretty much ended in a nice note. Everyone was petted, held, and fed, and that made us all happy once again.

Friday
Well, another sunny day. We went for our morning walk. I pooped in the same spot I did yesterday morning. Mary called me predictable. She said she has surprise for us later and off she went. I think someone still holds a grudge about yesterday. Who? Me? No, I will spell it so she doesn't know I am talking about her. L-u-c-y. She was still squeaking in the morning. Hey, I think that was the garage door. She's home, yeah. I will help you put Molly out. Who's that? It's Rick, Rick's here, yeah, someone else to play with me. Hey, it's Mary's step-son, Grant. I wonder if he likes animals. What is he doing? He got right in Molly's cage. Now, what is he doing? He is picking Lucy right up. Here I am, Rick, pet me, pet me.

Grant likes animals. He wants to take Lucy home. I told him it was okay with me, for that would mean more attention for me. Oh, come on, Mary let him take her. She keeps biting his ears. Now he's going upstairs to see Michael's lizards. I'll come with you. Hey, what are you doing now? Yuck, he's petting them. Come on, buddy, wash your hands before you touch me again. Come on, Grant, dinner is ready. I wonder what we are having tonight. Yummy steak! No, I am not picky really, any old piece will do. Hey, somebody throw me—the little guy—a bone. Yeah, little pieces, keep them coming. Throw some more in my dish. What's that? No, no I don't like cucumbers, good try, though. They left about 8 P.M. Mary cleaned up and I got a few more pieces of meat and then we went for our evening walk. There was a big dog and it was on a leash, but it was bucking like a horse. I just stood there watching. What was wrong with that dog? I should have gotten a treat just for being so good on the leash. I felt sorry for the other walker. I think he was embarrassed. I didn't move. I just stood there watching the fiasco. What, what do you want, oh, alright, come on, let's continue. Here, watch me, big guy, this is how it's done. Put one foot in front of the other. Show off! Hey, watch who you are calling a show off, Mary, or I'll start acting like that big dog over there. Once again, Molly's in her cage, Lucy is on Mary's chest and she is grinding her beak so she must be asleep. I'm on teddy. No, I am on the love seat. No, I've moved to the couch on top of all the pillows. It's time to go to sleep. See you in the morning.

Saturday

It's cloudy and raining. I'm not going for our walk, maybe later. Mary doesn't have to work so we get to hang out this morning. Everyone was fed and cleaned up. No, I don't mean me. I am always clean. Hey, watch who you're calling stinky. Alright, just put me in. I am getting a bath. Mary loves giving me a bath. She says I am ten times easier than those Golden Retrievers. Well, yeah, I am ninety lbs lighter. I am running around singing, I feel good, da, da, da, da, da. I've got my leash in my mouth and I am running all over the place. Mary's cleaning some of the rooms and now she's outside picking the dead flowers. I'll just cry a little to let her know I'm here. I am lying down and Mary's arm is about to fall off from working on the flowers. She told me to tell you that. We are going for a car ride later on, so I'll write later. Everyone is pretty content at the moment. Mary put Lucy in her cage and off we went for our walk. I miss all of you and I'm ready to see you again. I am going to go to bed and Mary said I'll get another surprise tomorrow, so goodnight.

Sunday

Another warm day. We were out on the patio this morning, all of us, Lucy, Sassy, and me. Mary was cleaning and packing. I was kind of sad. Where's my surprise? We had cereal for breakfast. We watched a movie and we played around a little. I don't mind when the suitcase comes, it's when it goes that it bothers me. Now, I am sitting on the patio rocker with Mary as she writes this all down. She seems sad today also. Hey, where are you going? And where is my surprise? Cry, cry, cry really loud. She can't hear me, but I know she knows I am crying. Ah, she left me a couple of treats. Okay, that's kind of nice, but where's my surprise? She must have forgotten. Yeah, she's

back! That's the garage door. Bark! Bark! Bark! Mom, Dad, you are all home. Yeah, great surprise. Thanks, Mary. Sit down, Mom, let me tell you about my week.
  Love,
  Chipper

Jo Ellen saved all the diaries that I had written to them. I thought this was great. It tells me that they actually meant something to them. It helped me remember all the great times that I had had with her animals.

Chipper had this horrific cry. I would be working outside and if he didn't see me go around the house he would instantly cry and I would have to peek around the corner and then he'd come running. It was just so funny to hear. It really did sound like he was in dire straights. It seemed to me that he was almost human.

If you knew him, you knew exactly what he was thinking just by the look on his face. .. I knew when he wanted a treat, when he wanted to go out to play or go for a walk. He was just that easy to read.

When he would go to Lane and Paul's, he would be really nervous at first. Then he seemed to relax when they ignored him. They would get too close to his nose and he would look at me as if to say, "Are you going to let them get that close to me?" He also seemed to feel very relaxed when we would all go for our walks, as if he was protected by the big dogs. He knew on the rides back to his home he would get a burger or ice cream, so the trips were well worth it.

(First, I can't believe you are putting this sweater on me with these big dogs watching me. They give me enough slack as it is, and second, are you really going to take my picture also?)

I think my favorite time was our time spent in the car. He would get in between the front seats and sit on the console. He was so tiny he fit perfectly and he could see everything. We would constantly look at each other while he was up there, and I would just smile and laugh. He seemed so human it was impossible for me to believe he was a dog. Not only did I get to see him every Tuesday when I cleaned, but I got to see him for all the family vacations. It was a time that I cherished whenever I was with him.

Chipper for a long time had bad skin allergies. Jo had him to several specialists to help him. It took her a long time to finally find someone that could actually help the little guy. It was hard to watch him lick his paws and chew so badly on his feet. You would have to ask yourself, is he in a lot of pain or is it just bothersome like humans when they have allergies? She finally found a doctor that helped him, but they weren't sure how long the treatments would work, but it did help at first. You just don't want your animal to suffer for any reason, so as long as the treatments were working they continued to take him to the doctors and let him live a normal life.

Times change and people's lives take different turns as kids get older. She didn't like leaving Chipper as he got older, so my time was not needed as much. I would run into Jo from time to time and learned they adopted a rescue dog, a Golden Retriever mix, Shadow. This doesn't surprise me that they rescued a dog. I remember one time I was cleaning their house and it was right around Christmas. On the dining room table, there were clothes and games and they all had a paper attached to them: Girl 14 needs this, Boy 9 needs size whatever. The table was full of toys and clothes in different piles. I asked Jo what that was all about and she said, "At Christmastime, there are trees in banks or churches or different stores that have all these tags with different names of boys and girls of all ages who are less fortunate and are in need of some help." So each of her kids picked out two or three tags and they went out and bought them whatever they had asked for on the tag plus some items they didn't ask for. Those children received gifts at Christmastime from Jo and her kids.. I remember thinking, I hope one day to have enough to do the same for others as Jo and her family had done. So it doesn't surprise me that she has a rescue dog, that's just the kind of person she is, not to mention the great lesson it taught her own children. Be thankful for all you have and to give to others when you can.

Jo noticed that Chipper was not responding to the treatments as well as he had previously. I think maybe his little body had taken all the medicine it could to help him get through life. One day she noticed he was in the kitchen and he was just crying that awful cry he had done so often to get my attention, and she understood completely what that was. You just know when it's time and Chipper was telling her it was time.

On May 3, 2006, Chipper slipped away at ten years old. Jo requested that Chipper be cremated and placed in a special urn. He now rests on top of her refrigerator, knowing that every time she opens it Chipper will still be there, as he always was.

In talking to Jo, she still has Shadow, and now she has a Maltese, Bella. Sassy passed away October 23, 2009 at the age of sixteen. Lucy is in an aviary where she is very happy. Lucy was Michael's and now that Michael is in college, Lucy was very sad so Jo had a friend that said she would take Lucy, and now she is with other birds and very happy again. She has a new bird and a new rabbit. Once again a house full of happy pets that, believe it or not, all get along great.

Thank you, Chipper, for all the happy memories.

Dolly

(Dolly on the bed watching me clean the bathroom)

Tuesday was my day to clean Chipper's house. One day, I was taking my cleaning supplies out to the car and I was getting barked at from across the street. You know me, I can't let a dog get away with that without saying hello. So I grabbed a Pupperoni from my car and walked across the street. I introduced myself and asked if the woman's dog would like a treat. Stephanie introduced herself and said, "Yes, Dolly, would love it." Dolly and I became instant friends. Dolly is a Silky Terrier, which would explain the barking. I should have known she owned the street. She was just letting me know from a distance how things were.

As our conversation continued, Stephanie asked if I had any time on my schedule to clean her house. I told her I definitely had time to clean as long as I was going to see this dog every week. On Tuesday morning, I cleaned for Jo and Chipper, and on Tuesday afternoons I cleaned for Stephanie and Dolly. Dolly followed me all over the house. I never dog sat for Dolly because she went everywhere with the family, but I bonded with Dolly every Tuesday. One day I was on my knees dusting in the living room and Dolly just jumped right on my back. She was so stinking cute. Anybody who has Terriers knows what a great personality they all have. Sometimes you just look at them and you question whether they are a dog or human. They know exactly what you are saying whether you are talking to them or about them.

(Yes, Mom, this is exactly where I am supposed to be!)

After two years of cleaning with Dolly, they moved to Florida. I was sad, but I knew that when I vacationed in Florida I would go and see her from time to time. A year passed since they moved, I was in Florida in July, and since they are close enough to the airport I called Stephanie and went to see them. I was afraid Dolly wouldn't remember me. I was wrong.

She was so excited she was jumping all around. She hadn't missed a beat with me. Stephanie took me around the neighborhood on their golf cart and Dolly sat on my lap the entire time. When we got back to the house, Stephanie offered me a glass of water. Dolly just looked at me, still on my lap as if she wanted something. Stephanie asked her if she wanted some water and said, "Come here, I will give you some water." She just looked at me, she wouldn't take water from Stephanie, so I offered her to drink some water from my glass, and don't you know it, she did. She couldn't drink it fast enough. Stephanie and I just laughed. She just looked at her and said, "Spoiled brat." I looked at her and kissed her little silky head.

So if you ever wonder if a dog will remember you if you leave for long periods of time, they will, and they never forget who loves them. They love you unconditionally, even if they are not yours.

(Who doesn't love a pretty face?)

Daisy

(Daisy at my mom's in Virginia for Christmas with her new toy)

My phone rang and on the other side of the line was a lady that would like me to start cleaning for her if I had the time. She got my name from her neighbor who I cleaned for on Fridays. So I met with Susan and quoted her a price for cleaning and immediately fell in love with her dog, a Maltese named Snowflake. I was happy to take her on as a cleaning client and I was to start the following Wednesday.

No one was home when I got there. Amelia, her daughter, was seven years old and was in school. There is no note as to where Susan is. I am looking all over for Snowflake and getting nervous because I can't find her anywhere. Then I was standing in the kitchen and I saw a bunch of balloons and a card. I read the card not to be nosy, but just a hunch. As I read the card it said, "I am so sorry about Snowflake." I had my answer as to why Snowflake was nowhere to be seen. I left Susan a note to call me and I found out that Snowflake had run into the road and was hit by a neighbor. Just an accident but I still felt badly both for Snowflake and the neighbor. I didn't really know Snowflake but was sad for Susan's loss just the same. I once hit a cat that was crossing the highway. There was no house around so I had no one to contact. I picked it up and took it to the hospital, but he was already gone. I felt terrible and I didn't even know the animal. I know you are not supposed to swerve to miss an animal on the road, but I always do. It's just an instinct to do so. Sometimes it works out and other times it doesn't. It's a terrible feeling to hit an animal with your car.

Not more than a month goes by and I walk into their house to find a little fluff ball named Daisy, who fits in the palm of my hand. She is a new little Maltese from the same breeder where Snowflake came from. It was my first Maltese puppy. I couldn't get enough of her. She was spunky even at eight weeks old. I carried her around everywhere I went in the house. Every Wednesday I got to cuddle and kiss this little puppy.

Susan was out of town for her job often. She's my computer geek. Actually, I am jealous she's so computer savvy. With her out of town so much, I got to spend a lot of time with Daisy. Plus, I would go over every day at lunchtime and take her for walks. On Wednesdays when she would see my cleaning bags, she then knew she was getting a doggie treat. She would dance around on her hind feet. She was really good at balancing for a long time to get her treat. I found out later that all Maltese will balance well on their two hind legs.

Like Chipper, I would take Daisy for rides and I would drive her out to my house, and like Chipper, she would poop as soon as she hit the dining room. I am not sure why these little dogs felt it necessary to christen my home but without fail every time. It was just the size of mini sausages not like a huge pile of poop in the middle of my living room, so I didn't freak out. I just knew Daisy was going to do that every time she entered my house.

Daisy would get into a lot of trouble as so many dogs do, and unfortunately we don't always catch them. When she was two, she got very sick. Susan took her to the vet and they had x-rays done. When Susan called me I couldn't believe what she was telling me. Daisy had eaten a sponge. The next statement just about killed me. She didn't know if Daisy was going to make it or not. Days of waiting and finally about a week later, we were seeing a slight improvement. For the first time we had a glimmer of hope that she would get through this. She was a sick little dog. She would just lie in Susan's arms when they would visit her at the hospital. I don't remember how long she was there, but it was a long time and when Susan finally brought her home, she was so weak and docile, not like herself at all. I wasn't convinced she was going to make it, and day by day she slowly came around. That was a very scary time for them. They just couldn't lose another dog so soon. It had to be good six weeks before Daisy was back to normal. Thank God.

We moved to another house with acres. Daisy loved running around the yard. Because we moved, I was able to put in a pool. Daisy didn't really like to get wet, but she loved to be with me always, so when I went in she went in. She would walk back and forth on the deck until I put her on the raft. She'd get her belly wet from the raft, but she was ok with that. She would just lay down and let me pull her around in the water. She would just lay there like she was queen of the pool, of course I was, but I never told her that.

(Queen Daisy as I like to call her)

As I said, Susan traveled frequently so I had Daisy as much as Susan did. I took her to my groomer, Lisa. She always looked so cute when she was first groomed, so clean until she'd roll in something then that was the end of that. I swear she did not like being clean. She loved being at home with Susan and Amelia, but she loved being with me just as much. Susan never felt bad for leaving her because she was just as happy to be with me as she was to be with Susan. You don't mind leaving your dog as long as you know they are with loved ones.

I would carry her around like a baby on my hip. That's where she was most comfortable. I swear she was half human just like all of my other little dogs. You knew what she was thinking at all times. She had that little dog mentality. If you asked her she would tell you she is a German Shepherd in a Maltese costume. She'd get around another dog and she would just bark and carry on like she was the biggest dog on earth. If you talk to people who have owned a Maltese, they would tell you they all have this mentality.

(Mom, me, and Daisy, everybody is hugging each other)

Susan would go to her mom's at Christmas, so Daisy would come and stay with us. That meant she was at Bright Eyes's with me. She would walk into the house like she owned it and she would see Bright and stop dead in her tracks. This is what I imagine she would say, "Holy cow, you are big. Maybe if I don't move, you won't notice I am here." She would let Bright sniff her and Bright would know she was too small to play with and go lay down. "That was close, now I can investigate the house." All was right with the world. It would be time to walk the dogs and they would all be very excited. Daisy would get out of Bright's way and we'd all go out. Daisy would wander off and Bright Eyes, being the mother hen that she was, would stay by her side and kind of push her towards me to keep her by me. It was quite endearing. Daisy would look up and see where we were and go on about her business with her nose to the ground until Bright Eyes would pull her back in. I am not sure why Bright felt responsible for her, but she did. Chip of course was always with us, and being a Beagle he had his own agenda. Chip, I am sure, said to himself when I would bring Daisy over, "Finally, a dog smaller than me," considering he was always surrounded by bigger dogs.

Daisy would drive up our driveway for her stay with us and she was so excited she knew she was going to get whatever she wanted for the next week or two. So, for days we would play with whatever toy she wanted, she ate whatever we were eating (not always the best thing to do, but we like to spoil her when we got her). She would go outside and stay with me, not that it mattered when we had 10 acres for her to run on, but she just stayed by my side and followed me around the gardens. In the morning, she would go out to do her business and just stand there and bark at the world, just making sure everyone knew she was awake and well. At night she would be in bed right along my side. Rick would go to work and that meant she got his pillow when he got out of bed. "Don't tell him." Daisy was top dog. She would go to work with me, she went everywhere I went. I was not allowed to leave the house without her.. She was just happy to be with us wherever we were.

When we went on vacation, I would bring Daisy back something. Since we didn't have kids, she was my child. She spent as much time with me as she did with Susan. I always told Susan we had joint custody, even though she paid the vet bills. Sometimes we would bring her special biscuits from a dog specialty shop, or a toy I saw in a store, or a scarf for her neck. I loved the scarves that Lisa would put on her after she got groomed. So if I found a scarf I liked, I would just pick it up. One time we went to Cancun and we brought her a sombrero just her size. It was so adorable we couldn't resist it. She was so good about wearing it. You could see it in her face she was thinking, "Okay, but if someone comes in, please take this off the top of my head. Thank you very much."

(Daisy's favorite time of the day. Morning under the covers.)

My mom loves dogs but not in her home, so when I would plan a trip to my mom's I would say, "I can't mom. I am watching Daisy." She would say, "Is that the little white one?" I knew what she was going to say next, "You can bring her," and off we would go down to mom's.

Daisy was used to riding back and forth to Susan's mom's house in Kentucky, so I knew she would ride well. She would move around in the back and then come and sit in my lap when she got restless, or she just wanted to watch out the window. Then we would get to mom's and she would act like she owned the place. She would run around and go for walks then play fetch with my dad. Nighttime would come and she was right in bed with us. My mom is such a softie. It's not that she doesn't like dogs. She had six or more growing up, but it would just break her heart when they died. So she didn't want to get attached to any more dogs. It was safer that way. But for Daisy, she always made an exception for. As I said before, Daisy was my child. That meant she was her grand dog. She had to love her.

Days passed into years. Daisy went through so many changes with her owner and her dog sitter. Susan went through a divorce and she moved across town. She had a new home that she adapted quite easily to. However, with Susan moving she no longer needed me to clean. I was a luxury she couldn't quite justify. I completely understood and I still watched Daisy when Susan went away. I often watched Amelia and Daisy. Amelia and I became closer than ever. You know what I say: When a door is closed, God opens a window. I believe things happen for a reason. We don't always see the reason right away but it does come to us. That's when you say to yourself, "Oh, yeah, that makes sense now," or just one day you see the bigger picture. By this time, Amelia was in the eighth grade and because she was in school, I would come to her house and watch her and Daisy. I loved these days. I would wake up and walk Daisy while Amelia would get ready for school. She was such a great student she was easy to watch. I didn't have to bother her to do her homework I knew it was always done. She loved going out to dinner and she was in bed early so that left nighttime to just Daisy and me. We would watch TV downstairs and play with the ducky, her favorite stuffed toy. Then it was off to bed, our favorite time together. She would start in the middle of the bed then by the time we fell asleep she was on the pillow next to my head. All was right with the world.

(She loved her sombrero, I should have gotten myself one as well)

Over the next two years, Rick and I would become divorced and Daisy went through another house change with me. She adapted well again to all the changes. At this point I was dating Mark and we lived in Erie. Daisy would stay with us and we have a fenced in yard, so she would stand by the door when she wanted to go outside. She would just stand out there and bark at trees, leaves, shadows, anything she could, just to hear her own voice. Then she would race in and go right to the kitchen for a treat. I was not sure what she's thinking, but I could only imagine if I knew Daisy, it would be something like this: "Okay, I went out and saved the world with my barking. Now, where's my treat?" It was like clockwork.

Amelia and Daisy would come and stay with us when Susan was gone. Amelia was now in Senior High and at the same school with Mark's son, Jesse. Amelia and Mark were inseparable. He would take them both to school and pick her up. Jesse always had some school activity or football, so it was just Amelia and Mark coming home from school. Daisy would often go with me to work if she could, and if I was at a house that she couldn't go to, I would guilt Mark into taking her with him to the bowling alley. She loved going there. She would run up and down the carpet. As soon as she went into the building, she would go right for the kitchen for some small pieces of ham and water. She would follow Mark everywhere. One time she went on the lanes and passed the foul line. Mark yelled at her and told her she could go anywhere except past the foul line, and do you know that dog was so smart she never ever went past the foul line again. She would go down the sides of the lanes into the back if Mark had to work on a machine. She loved the senior lady bowlers and would say hello to all of them. Once there was a young family in for open bowling, and the little girl about three years old wanted to pet Daisy. If Daisy thought she could take someone down, she did so. So this was a prime time for Daisy. She ran up to the three year old and knocked her down and Daisy jumped on her and was getting really friendly with her, if you know what I mean. She didn't hurt the little girl. She was actually laughing and Daisy was just showing her a little love.

One time, Mark took her for a ride while he was running some errands getting supplies for the bowling alley. He had gone into the meat market and then he went to get some more supplies. Much to Mark's disappointment, Daisy would jump up on the doors to watch where he was going. Unfortunately, this particular time she locked the doors with the keys inside it. Daisy, at this time, decided to go exploring while Mark tried to figure out how to get the car unlocked. He's watching Daisy as she slowly went to the back of the van where he placed the food from the market. He just said to himself, "Don't do it, Daisy." He looked at her and said, "Bad dog." She looked up at him in that devious way she looked at you when she was about to do something she knew she was going to get in trouble for, and then she started to eat the ham. There wasn't anything Mark could have done.

By the time AAA got there to unlock the door, she had devoured all the ham. He just looked at her as she came up to the front seat licking her lips and he said, "I hope you throw up." Then back to the meat market for more ham. Guess what happened on the way back to the bowling alley? Yep, you guessed it, she threw up all over the back of the van. Needless to say, Mark was not very happy with Daisy. I just picked her up and said, "Ah, are you alright?" I tried to tell her ham isn't good for dogs, but given the chance, I do believe she would do it all again. I am not sure Mark appreciated the fact that I felt it necessary to laugh when he told me what she had done. But to hear him tell the story, I could picture how the whole incident went down.

Susan decided to take a trip abroad with her mom, and Amelia had school so once again, she and Daisy stayed with Mark and me. Amelia is such a smart girl, but as Mark would put it, "a true blonde." Please don't take offense to this remark. Amelia would always laugh at this comment and she too would agree. When I say she was smart, I mean top of her class smart. Amelia was on the rowing team so she had to be at the lake pretty early. They would row before school. She was an early riser so this fit her schedule really well. Me, I would still be in bed when they left; I am not a morning person. But she would come back into the house at least two or three times because she would forget things. No, I mean all the time. She would make her lunch and leave it in the fridge. Her book bag would be on the floor and she would have to come in and get that. Then it was her gym bag she forgot. Really, almost every day it was something. Mark and I would just shake our heads and then we would all laugh. Mark absolutely loves this girl. They were so close, and Daisy and I would just snuggle up together in bed while Amelia would come back and forth. These are the days I fondly remember.

Daisy would spend a lot of the holidays with us. She was getting older and didn't much care to travel in the car as she did when she was younger. She would get along with whatever dog I had at the time just as long as I knew she was top dog. I would tell her that, but then look at the other dogs and shake my head no behind her back. What, it was always behind her back so she never knew what I was saying. It was Christmas and for the first time I was at home for the holidays and not with Bright and PT. My parents came and Daisy was here as well.. My dad just loved Daisy. They would play for hours then she would snuggle in the chair with my mom. She loved Christmastime with us for she knew she was going to get new toys and treats.

I had taken Daisy every five weeks, for about the last eight years now, to get her groomed. This was really the only time I spend with Daisy now. Susan is home most of the time working out of her house, so our time with Daisy is limited. Amelia is graduating from high school in a month. Oh, how the time flies by. It seems just like yesterday she was in grade school. Susan has decided since Amelia is attending the University of Louisville, and her mother lives in Kentucky, she too would move back home to be closer to her family. This meant that I was going to be missing a whole lot of people in my life: Susan, Amelia and Daisy.

Amelia and Jesse were in the same school and grade. It was now Graduation day. There were also some of Mark's employees graduating from that same school, so we knew a lot of kids from that graduation class. Knowing so many kids it made that day extra special. Amelia didn't want a graduation party; she wanted her family to go out to dinner to celebrate, so that's what they did. We met up with them after dinner for a few cocktails and laughs. Actually a lot of laughs. We told Amelia she had to keep in contact with us so we knew everything was okay..

(Daisy and Mark on Christmas day, notice Chelsea's head with her new Christmas toy in her mouth)

This summer was hectic for Susan. She had her house on the market and was getting her new house ready for the move. I kept Daisy for her, so that was one less detail she had to worry about. I knew my time with Daisy was limited and I enjoyed every minute I could with her. Through the years, we had been through a lot and I wouldn't have changed a thing. I knew that I would see them again and that they would be back for visits to see friends and family. It wouldn't be the same as driving down the street five minutes to visit them, but I would have to be okay with that. All I can do is give hugs and kisses and wish them well, and thank them for all the memories.

Amelia comes home from college for holidays and over the summer to see her relatives and close friends back here, and like a good daughter, she always calls us to go to dinner or just to come over and hang. We pick up right where we left off laughing and talking about the good times. Sometimes she brings Daisy and even her mom. The last time they were in town, they had so much to do we didn't get to see them, which was sad. I am hoping for a summer visit. Amelia is in her second year of college and loving it. Susan is thinking about going back to school herself, always learning more this one. Daisy is typical Daisy. She is now 14 years old and still going strong. My husband has a saying that he always says when you are leaving the bowling alley, "Miss you when you are gone." So to Susan, Amelia and Daisy, "We miss you when you are gone." But we will see you soon.

Dinkey

One Christmas, my girlfriend Connie and her husband decided the kids were old enough to have a dog, so they decided on a tiny black cocker spaniel. It was snowing pretty good on Christmas Eve and they picked the dog up around 2 P.M. on the east side of town and drove him way over to the west side to my house. Dinkey would stay with us till the kids were asleep and it was safe for them to come and get him.

Of course, the first thing he does is pee on my dining room carpet. Once again my carpet is christened. But he is so cute I can't even get mad. I just cleaned it up and become a little more diligent about taking him outside more often. He was this little black ball of fur. We bonded right away, or at least I had hoped. I figured I would be seeing this dog a lot. I was godmother to Connie and Tom's son Kristopher, so I guess, I assumed I would be seeing Dinkey grow up, so bonding was definitely in the cards for us. I was sleeping on the couch when they came to pick him up and I was sad to see him go, but he wasn't my Christmas gift so I handed him over to Connie reluctantly. I could only imagine what the kids would be like when they came down their stairs to see him. Christmas morning and Connie said the kids flew down the stairs to see all their gifts. The puppy was behind the tree and they didn't even see him. Then he slowly crept around the corner of the tree and the kids went wild. They named him Dinkey.

Over the next couple of years, I fell madly in love with this little guy. I was not sure what it was but there was a bond there. Then one day, because of Tom's job, they were moving to Toledo. That didn't stop Connie's friends from visiting her, so off to Toledo, Michelle and I would go. As soon as we walked in the house, Dinkey boy would stick to me like glue. I got to sleep in Kristopher's room and I wasn't ever alone. Any other time Dinkey would sleep with Tom and Connie, except when I was in the house, he slept with me. I loved it, even though he drooled. I probably did too, but he never complained. No matter what house he was in I was the person to be with. Connie was a close second because she was the one who fed him, but I was number one when I was with him.

They then moved to Baltimore. The kids were getting older and Brandie was in college. Michelle and I didn't care where we slept. We didn't want to put the kids out, but I don't think they cared so much it was like having a sleepover in the basement. I often slept in Courtney's room in the single bed and once again I wasn't alone. Dinkey would sleep at my feet. He would start at my head but by the time morning came around, he was at my feet. One time we came in really late coming home from a trip to Myrtle Beach, so instead of waking the kids, Michelle and I slept on the sofa bed, except Dinkey crawled up in between us and Michelle said no way she was sleeping with the dog. Like I said, he was a drooler. Michelle loved Dinkey also but not enough to sleep with him. She lost. She slept in the chair. No I didn't feel guilty. Can I just say that when Michelle stays with my dog when I am out of town, she lets her sleep with her in the bed. Go figure. I was not going to kick Dinkey out of bed. I cherished what little time we had together.

Tom's parents still lived in Erie so they would come home to visit often and they would stay with us. Dinkey would come in and most often I would have another dog here for him to play with, so it was fun for him. It would be for a long weekend, but it was great to have everyone here. It was like old times. They finally made their last move to Virginia. Dinkey was getting older now. If ever there was a dog that was a big part of the family, Dinkey was definitely one of them. He went everywhere. He came to Erie, he would go to Connie's home town in Winchester, VA to visit her mom and her brother and sister. Her parents' dog is Cuddles. Cuddles and Dinkey spent a lot of time together so they were inseparable.

From Erie to Toledo, to Baltimore and finally to Virginia. Dinkey was the youngest of Connie and Tom's kids. I say that because he was such an important part of the family as are most dogs Connie, for a long time was a stay-at-home mom, so they were together all the time. He was happiest when everyone was home together. He was in every family portrait, and snapshot he could be in. Everywhere the family went he went also. That was Dinkey in a nutshell.

When I got the call from Connie, I knew something was wrong. You can always tell when she has been crying, she would start the conversation, "Mary," and when it was just a normal phone call I would get, "Hi, Mar." So I knew something was wrong. Now there have only been a few times that I can recall that she had called me with bad news, and I always hated that "Mary" because I knew it wasn't going to be good. She told me that Dinkey was sick that he had a tumor on his bowel. I of course asked if it was operable and she said she didn't think so, so they were going to biopsy it and then she would know more. But at this particular time she just needed someone to tell her he was going to be okay, which, you know, was me. "You caught it early. Don't get upset until there is something to be upset about." You know how upset you are until you talk to someone else that you hope will be the voice of reason or at least calm you down so you can think clearly. Well, that was this phone call. She was calmer when she hung up but you knew this was going to be a strain on the family. I told her to keep me posted.

We found out that it was not operable and that the outcome was not good. So at this point what do you say? All I could say was, "Love the time you have with him, let him know he is not alone and kiss him every chance you get." As the weeks wore on he went downhill fast, and as you can imagine it was killing the whole family. They were so far away and all I could do was console her from a distance. I would have loved to have been there for her and Dinkey, but some things were just out of my reach. I knew of course that Dinkey knew I loved him because I never left without telling him how I felt, so I was okay with letting him go. It is easier when you are not there to see him and hold him.

Dinkey passed away in August, devastating the family he had left behind. I will never forget his loving little black furry face and those beautiful eyes that always melted me when he looked at me. Dinkey had a wonderful life with Connie and Tom and the kids, not a better home could he have found. Goodbye my truly lovable little friend that I loved and whom loved me no matter how many miles apart we were.

Abby

One day, I got a call for a cleaning job for Ronnie and Dick. I pulled up to this really big home and I was greeted by a very happy Golden Retriever, Abby. She is so sweet. She didn't jump on me as Bright and PT would have, later finding out she was trained not to jump or lick anyone. She was so well behaved. As I was walking through the house so I could give Ronnie an estimate as to how much it would be for me to clean, I noticed a picture on their mantle of 13 or 14 golden pups. I asked if one was Abby and she said yes, and then I find out they had her brother as well, but Zach got out of the invisible fencing and was killed by a car. I felt sad for Abby and instantly thought of PT and Bright, how one would be lost without the other.

I took the cleaning job for Ronnie and instantly became best buds with Abby. They had invisible fencing outside and inside the house. She wasn't allowed in the good living room or the dining room, so she followed me to all the other rooms as I cleaned. She was my blonde shadow.

They asked me to dog sit for them and I was happy to do that. I would sit so close and look her right in the face, and she would never kiss me. That's how trained she was. I mean, literally, I would stick my face in hers because I love doggy kisses and to no avail, she wouldn't do it. I tempted her constantly. If I even looked at Bright or PT they'd go nuts on my face, no, not like "Something about Mary dog scene." They would just lick my face, but Abby never would. I had never seen anything like it ever.

It was a rainy Saturday at her house and we stayed in and watched movies all day. I remember I was watching a story about a wolf, and Abby went crazy, she'd go right up to the TV screen and sit right in front of it. She was actually watching TV. She loved wolves and other dogs. She was just the sweetest golden. I know they are all sweet, but I am partial to all my goldens that I watch. She spent most of her time in the great room and kitchen. She'd sleep right next to the bed. I'd try and coax her into the bed (Don't tell Ronnie because she wasn't allowed in the bed), but being the good girl she was, she would never get on the bed. I was amazed at how well behaved she was at all times. Even when she could be bad she wasn't. She was your dream dog.

One time I took her for a car ride, backed out of the driveway and she yelped like mad, so that's when I realized that I didn't take her electric collar off of her. I completely forgot it and I felt awful. I was so upset I drove her right up to Creamland and got her a vanilla cone. She forgave me, and yes I took it off of her before I drove back into the driveway. I can honestly say I never did that again.

One Sunday, I was doing a special cleaning for Lane. I finished the house before anyone got home from the funeral, said goodbye to the dogs and drove home. At about 8:30 P.M. my phone rang and it was Lane. I thought maybe I had missed something or did something wrong, and after talking to her I wish it was just that but it wasn't. PT had been in an accident and didn't make it. I remember being perfectly silent on the phone. I immediately thought of Bright and how I didn't kiss them before I left and tell them that I loved them. Lane said to me, "Mary, did you hear me?" I told her yes, and asked her if there was anything I could do for them. I told her how sorry I was that they had lost PT. From that moment on, I'd never leave a house without letting each dog know that I love them and they always get a kiss because you just never know. I want them to know how I feel at all times. I didn't get that chance with PT, and I will never let that happen ever again. I felt badly for Lane and Paul, and then thought how was Bright Eyes going to be without her brother and best friend. I would find out soon enough.

Monday, I was with Abby and thought how lonely she must have been without Zach. I remember kissing her for no reason and it didn't matter that she didn't kiss me back, even though I could have used it, she knew that I loved her. I began to cry uncontrollably for the first time for PT and didn't stop for days.

Abby had a big dog house in the garage that led to the outside. It was actually pretty cool. At first I thought how sad that she had to go out to the garage while Ronnie and Dick were at work, but she had a big dog bed in it and because it led to the outside by a trap door, she could go outside whenever she wanted to. So actually this was a very cool thing she had going on. When I was dog sitting her, as soon as I got home from work, she ran right into the house, and she would run into the great room as if she was going to miss her favorite TV program. I would sit on the floor with her because of course she wasn't allowed on the furniture, so it was the floor for me as well. As I am reading this back it sounds like she had a lot of rules and wasn't allowed to do anything. On the contrary, she was just a well-trained dog, very loved by Ronnie and Dick and myself.

She loved going into the backyard and she would just sit there while I brushed her. She loved getting brushed and groomed. I suspect it feels much like a great massage.. She had this thick tooth comb that really got to her undercoat. We could make a new dog with all the hair I combed off of her. I find that most Goldens love to be brushed and pampered, and she was no exception to the rule.

One time, I took Abby for a walk, closed the door behind us and came back to a locked door. Oops. I went next door in hopes that they possibly had a key to their neighbor's house. Believe it or not, they did. His name was George and his wife was Barb. I thanked him and the next day I had a key made and hid it outside just in case I ever did that again. I wonder if the key is still there. Probably, I hid it well.

We'd go for car rides and walks often. She loved to do both. One time, I was cleaning the master bathroom and I had the TV on. At one point she was in front of it just watching it as she often did, and in the next second she was walking nervously around as if she was watching a scary movie and she just couldn't watch anymore. I changed the channel and she went right back to sitting in front of it to watch. I am not making this up. I found this to be odd, so I put it back to the movie and sure as I was standing there she was disturbed and got right back up and started to pace back and forth. It was a western movie and horses were running wild. I changed the channel and the same thing happened again. She loved wolves and dogs, but not horses. They freaked her out. Don't tell me that dogs don't see the TV and what's on because she proved it to me right then. From that moment on if there was any program with horses on, I watched and the same thing would happen, she would get up and pace back and forth. From time to time just to check out my theory, I would put horses on, and she would never disappoint me. She would always get up and walk away from the TV. I would quickly change the channel so it wouldn't upset her too much.

Every now and then, I would notice she had a cough. I asked Ronnie about it and she told me Abby did have a heart murmur or something to that effect. You would never know it because she was always so happy-go-lucky all the time, never showing a sign that there might be a problem. She was always running in the backyard, going up and down the stairs. I never gave her any medication when I watched her, but that didn't mean she wasn't on any at any time.

One night, I got a call from Ronnie. Abby was having a hard time breathing so Ronnie put her in the car and by the time she had driven her to the hospital, she had passed away. As I write this, I begin to tear up. Ronnie told me her heart just gave up. Ronnie was crying as she was talking to me and I was crying right along with her. It was a long night with my thoughts of Abby.

That night, I went to bed with tears in my eyes and a very heavy heart, which caused me to dream. In my dream, Abby was in it and she was standing next to me. As I was sleeping I was telling myself, "See, Abby isn't gone, but that it was a dream that Ronnie called me," and as I bent down to pet her she jumped up and licked my face. I woke up and realized at that moment Abby had come to me in my dream to say goodbye. In the dream, she licked my face then just faded away. Remember, she never licked me, ever, except this particular night and then she was gone.

The next day, I sat in Ronnie's kitchen with her and told her about the dream. It was so vivid I still remember it as if it were yesterday. It has been at least ten years since Abby has been gone and I still can't write about this or talk about this dream without sobbing. Abby is still the only dog I have ever dreamed about. I loved her and miss her terribly and hope to see her one day again.

I lost two Goldens in one year. That is two too many in my eyes. Each Golden Retriever has taught me lessons along the way and I will love them forevermore.

Sami

Remember when I locked myself out of Abby's house and I had to go next door to see if maybe they would have a key and lucky for me they did? Well, that was George and Barb. Barb had asked Ronnie who I was and if she had liked my cleaning job, and then I got a call from Barb to start cleaning for her and her family. Nice people, lived right next to Abby so I could go over and see her whenever I was working at Barb and George's. It was a win-win situation. I was happy to be working for George and Barb. They had two girls in junior high, Susan and Beth. They had had a Golden Retriever about four years earlier that had passed away, so I was just there to clean. Barb was a stay-at-home mom and she was busy with taking care of her family. Her house was beautifully decorated and I enjoyed cleaning for them very much. When I would first get to the house, I would start in the girls' bathroom and Barb would sit on the stairs that were directly across from the bathroom. We would catch up on what happened the previous week and then she would go on her way and let me do my job. She often talked about getting another dog, but wasn't sure if the family was ready.

One year into cleaning for them, I came into the house and low and behold, a puppy was in the kitchen to greet me. She was so stinking cute, a beautiful tri-colored Sheltie named Sami. Sami was glued to Barb. It took her a few Mondays to get used to me, but after that we were best friends. Barb always took Sami for car rides to pick up the girls or go run errands. Those two were inseparable. She was six months old and still she didn't have the mane that Shelties have, and Barb was worried that maybe something was wrong. So I told Barb to call the breeder that they got her from to ask. She did and found out they don't get that full coat until they are at least one year old. I learn something new every day.

Sami was my first experience with Shelties. She was a talker. She played and barked and played and barked every minute of every day. She loved to talk to everyone. They had an invisible fence for her and she talked to everybody that walked by. If you have ever watched any of the dog shows, you know that they give you a detailed description of the breed as they are being judged and the one thing they always say about the Shelties is that they are very big talkers. Sami was very vocal, so if you are trying to decide on a puppy for your family, always watch the dog shows and the announcers can pretty much pick out a dog that fits your family because they are right on the mark with their descriptions of the dogs. Shelties are the friendliest dogs, the most loyal of dogs, great with children, strangers and friends alike. Strangers would be leery of her because she was so vocal they didn't know if she was mean or not. They didn't know she was saying, "Hey, I don't know you, but I would like to. You look like a great person to get to know. So come on over here and pet me."

Sami knew when I would come that it was treat time. She would greet me at the door, and patiently sit for her "Pupperoni." As usual, I would start upstairs and Barb would sit there and talk to me while Sami sat in front of her to get her usual rubdown. Sami would always bring me a toy, and I would throw the toy and she would bring it right back to me. She would do this all day if I let her, but I had to work and Barb would call her and she would go running downstairs to play with Barb so I could work. Sami's favorite toy, oh heck, they were all her favorite toys, but I think she likes the tennis ball the most.

Sometimes, when they went on vacation I would bring Sami to my house and sometimes I'd stay at hers. They were gone one year for Thanksgiving for a long weekend so I brought her to my house. We got so much snow that weekend I had to shovel the deck so she could have a path to get to the yard. She loved the snow. She would go crazy when I picked up the shovel. She would bark as if to say, "Throw it my way, I'll catch it, really I will." She would bark at me and I would throw it in the air and it would just fall in her face. The more snow the better. She loved coming to my house as much as I loved going to hers. It didn't matter where she was as long as I was with her.

(Sami telling me to throw the snow in the air)

George and Barb decided to go to Ireland for three weeks, so I stayed at her house for those three weeks. She slept on the bed with me. She had her own bed that she would sleep in normally, but because it was just me she'd just curl up in bed with me and go to sleep. She didn't move all night and I loved having her next to me. It was the same thing every day. Get up, go for a walk, eat breakfast and play for about an hour. I would take her with me to wherever I was as long she was welcomed to do so. Other than that, Sami would wait for me to get home from my day at work.

Sami would bring me a toy and place it right in my lap or drop it at my feet. Relentlessly. If she wasn't sleeping she was playing. My nephew's high school graduation party was on a Saturday, so I decided to take her to New York for the day. She was so excited on the car ride, which was a long one for her. When she got to the party she ran around like it was her own backyard.

She was so good, she greeted everyone with a hello in hopes that they would stop and talk to her, which everyone did. She was hard to ignore. She played with the tennis ball with anyone who would play with her and she got to eat some hamburgers. When we played badminton she decided to play with us, often grabbing the birdie and running away with it. Everyone would stop to chase her and this became her favorite game. It was late June so it was pretty warm, especially with her thick coat so she often took breaks drinking water and finding shade under the picnic table.

There was a little baby probably no more than five months old there and she was in her car seat the whole time. Tina asked me if the dog was good with children. I honestly said I've never seen her with babies before, but my honest opinion would be yes, she would be good with the baby. So she put the car seat down near the picnic table and Sami came right over to the baby. I was cautious, and then Sami sniffed the baby then licked her little face. The answer was yes, she is good with babies. Sami slept the whole way home. She was exhausted and curled up on my lap in the front seat. She had had a wonderful day in New York.

I came to just love, love, love this dog. We went on walks morning, noon and night. On Mondays and Thursdays, she would go to Lane and Paul's with me. When we first arrived there she would say hi to Bright then she would start her ritual of running from tree to tree barking and chasing the birds out of one into another. She loved to be here because she had lots of room to roam. This would continue for an hour or so. When she got tired she would run into the house, get a drink and bring me the tennis ball while I was trying to work. I would throw it a couple of times and then she would go back outside to chase the birds and squirrels again.

Sami got along with everyone, Bright and Chip liked her, but they were exhausted just watching her run around. I would watch from a window and you could just see their heads following Sami as she barked and chased the creatures that were scampering around. If I dared to guess what she was thinking it would be this, "Oh, my God, you have so much property to run around on, come on, guys, play. Look at all these trees, oh, there is a bird. Where do you think you are going? Oh, look, there goes one, there over there to this tree to that tree. Oh, my, so much land to run, run and run." See what I mean? It was just exhausting.

When I was done cleaning for the day, I always took them for a walk. They knew when I was done they would all be sitting there looking at me and I would say, "Walk?" They would instantly be up and on their way. Chip would look back and with his butt going back and forth with excitement would lead the pack. Bright would start out with a little trot then come to my side to walk by me. Sami of course would be barking, "Yeah, a walk. Come on faster, let's go." She would be off and running a little ahead of us. They all loved their walks.

(Bright, Chelsea, and Sami on one of our many walks)

She loved coming to Paul and Lane's, but I tell you, she was so tired when we got home, there was no playing. It was just eat dinner and lay on the couch, watch movies with me by my side and fall asleep. That is how much running around she would do, so tired she couldn't keep her eyes open. There were days she was sore the next morning, she would be slow getting up.

I had one more weekend with her and then the family would be home on Sunday. I decided to take her for a car ride and get my car washed. Not one of my better choices. We got caught at a train crossing on the way to the car wash and she barked the entire time the train was passing us by. She doesn't like trains. Then we got to the car wash and guess what, yep, barked through the whole process. The machine would start on the driver's side and she'd be at that side, then to the back window, over to her side and back up to the front seat. She was clawing at my dashboard barking at the machine. I was half tempted to put the car windows down so she would get sprayed, but decided to suck it up and not ever take her to a car wash ever again. Who knew?

Three weeks went by so fast, I was sorry to leave her. We had such a great time. Sami was happy to see her family and they were just as happy to see her. Barb was grateful that she didn't have to worry about Sami at all. They had a great time in Ireland, but probably not as fun as Sami and I had. I wasn't too sad because I knew I would be back on Monday to clean and play with my friend once again.

We were back to our regular schedule of seeing each other on Mondays. She didn't go to Lane and Paul's with me because every minute was spent with Barb. I loved seeing her and she was just as excited to see me. We had a great bond, as I often did with so many of my dogs. She was right up there at the top of my list. It's been two years now and I get to watch Sami whenever the family goes on vacation or just does a weekend trip. This was my favorite time of the year, every Monday when I clean and every time the family goes away. Life was good for Sami and myself.

One day in August, I was cleaning and Barb had asked me something. She was in the great room and I was in the kitchen so I didn't hear what she said so I said, "What?" She sat down and just started crying. I said, "Barb, I didn't hear what you said. What's wrong?" She said she didn't know. She'd gone to the doctor's office because recently she was slurring her words and she didn't know why. That's why I didn't understand what she had said because the words didn't come out right. The doctor's office was so busy she had to leave before being seen because she had to pick up the kids from school. I told her to make another appointment that I would pick up the girls from school. She made the appointment and on August 28, I got a call from George; my friend had a brain tumor. The size of the tumor was quite large. They operated the next day, and after the operation George called again and asked me if I could help with Sami. No need for him to even ask that.

I came to the house every day at noon. Sami and I would walk around the neighborhood. Sami loved her walks. She would walk until we came to a house where she knew there was a dog. I mean she knew every house that contained a dog. She would get close to the house and start tugging on the leash. She would bark all the way by the house calling each of them out or at least to come to the door. Down the street there was a little Bichon Frise that almost always sat on the window sill. I swear that little dog knew we would be coming because he was always there. But as soon as we would round the corner, Sami was barking and this little white fluff ball would be barking back at us and the owner would just wave to me, knowing it was me every day. Sami would go nuts barking and running up and down on her leash, then we would move on to the next house. Down the street a little further we would come to a yellow Lab, Bailey, who would always be out in the front yard waiting for our arrival. Bailey was in an invisible-fenced yard, so he would also just stand there and talk to Sami as we walked by. I swear it was just like in those movies where the dogs all talk and Bailey was saying, "Hey, girl, looking good today, nice day for a walk." Sami would bark back and say, "Why don't you come out of that driveway and walk with us. I would like that a lot. Okay, have to go now and see who's left. See you tomorrow, Bailey." Rounding the corner there was a black Lab, Bucky, who also had the invisible fencing and he would just sit up, take note of Sami's presence, and then lay back down. Then finally to the "piece de resistance," you know what I mean—the final–Sami's favorite dog, the handsome miniature Schnauzer, Max.

Max was one dog that Sami knew he could call to come outside. She would start barking two houses before and you would see Max run to the front door. Most times, Max was already outside waiting for Sami in his front yard. Max also had invisible fencing and I knew the two dogs got along, so I would walk Sami up the driveway and Max would be cautious and run up to sniff Sami. This became a ritual. If Max was out we would always stop to say hi then it was on our way back home. Barb's sister, Gloria, came to stay with Barb after the surgery to take care of her in her recovery, so I was in charge of Sami. On Tuesdays and Thursdays I would just come and pick up Sami and take her to Lane and Paul's, which she loved, and the rest of the week I would just come and walk her.

One day I sat down with George and we talked. Sadly, Barb was given a year to live. As you can imagine George couldn't even think straight, so he was going to need some help from all of us. Gloria I think stayed with Barb and the family for six or eight weeks. Mike, Gloria's husband, would come up on weekends to be with his wife and the family. He's a pretty funny guy, and everyone could use a laugh, so he was great to have around. I took on one more day of cleaning for them, so I was at the house every Monday and Friday. After two months, Barb had fully recovered from the surgery. They had removed the tumor but we knew it was just a matter of time before it would grow back. In the meantime, life continued on. She continued to drive the girls to school and their activities. And to the outsider it was life as usual, to the family and close friends it was precious time.

I remember one day it was snowing out, it was a Saturday, and I got a call from Barb. This was strange because I see her so much during the week I instantly thought something was wrong. We never really talk about her illness; we would just carry on our days as if it were just another day. So when the phone rang, it startled me. I said hello and there was just silence. So I said, "Barb" and she started to speak. I could tell she was crying. I asked her if she was okay, was anything wrong and she said no. So I asked her again, "Talk to me." Up to this point Barb had never said, why me? She started talking and said her head hurt a little like a headache, but not a migraine. She had medicine but didn't want to take it if she didn't have to. She needed to relieve some of the stress of it all so she needed an ear. She said her biggest problem with this illness was not dying, but it was leaving the girls. I told her if I could switch places with her I would. I didn't have children to leave behind, I told her I had often asked God why and then all of a sudden she was consoling me. She said to me, "No. God has his reasons and we don't ask why, this is my fate and you have yours. You just don't know what that is yet." This was the one and only time she had ever asked, why her? She said thank you for talking. She needed that and I said, "See you on Monday." I remember this conversation like it was yesterday. I had been standing at my dining room sliding-glass door looking out over the backyard watching the snowfall.

I would always know what kind of day Barb was having because I would pull up the driveway and most often on the bad days, she and Sami would be sitting on the step and she would look at me and say, "Creamland," and the three of us would go to get ice cream and hopefully not run into a train when we went because of Sami, of course. All three of us would get a cone.

As time went on Barb did her usual everyday things, like decorating the house, the shopping and taking care of Sami and the girls. George was home early some days just to spend time with Barb, and it used to drive her nuts. She needed life to be as normal as possible and he needed to be with her. I sided with George and told Barb to suck it up and enjoy the special attention, then she would just stick her tongue out at me. I gave it right back to her. Barb loved to cross stitch and she did beautiful work, but she found out that she couldn't see the small stitches anymore so that upset her, but it didn't stop her, so she just started other crafts. I hated her for this particular gift she had, to be able to do such great craft work. She decorated the house so wonderfully, I was jealous. She had a knack of making the house a very warm place to be. She spent almost all of her time with Sami during the day, playing and just enjoying time together. Then time with the whole family at night.

(Beth, Barb, George, Susan and Sami up front)

Susan was turning 16 and they decided to throw her a sweet-sixteen party. Barb was trying to make sure she was thinking of everything for the girls. This was her biggest concern, for she knew George was going to be okay, but she was just exhausted thinking of what she wanted the girls to know. She often told me the one thing she was most upset about was not being able to watch the girls grow to be young women. She said they knew her as a mom, but they wouldn't know her as their best friend. This bothered her the most. I remember when my own mother and I became friends. Growing up she was my mortal enemy, then I turned 19 and I finally got it. All those years of discipline and controlling was for my own good. After that she was my best friend and to this day still is. Thank God for good mothers. So I understood exactly what Barb was saying and I felt terribly sad for her. They bought Susan a car for her birthday so she could help with the driving. Beth would turn sixteen in August and she wasn't sure how she would be at that time, so she took Beth out in the summer before she turned sixteen to teach her to drive. So many things she wanted them to know, but how do you know what's most important? What do you teach them and what do you let them learn on their own? By the end of the summer, she stopped trying to teach and just loved them as much as she could, realizing this is what they needed the most.

Sami was never far from Barb's side ever. I think she knew something was up, but just didn't know what it was. Barb was taking more naps during the day and Sami was right next to her at all times. I continued to take her for her walks and she would run back in the house and go right to Barb's side. Dogs just know.

Barb tried every new drug that she could. Any experiment to shrink the tumor which was growing back by this time. They even spent time at Duke University trying everything that medical science had to offer. George too was always reading and trying to find a cure for her, but to no avail, and by September, a year and a month after she was first diagnosed, Barb was in the final stages of her cancer. She asked three things of me: Make sure I continue to clean two days a week; help the girls get through high school and whatever they need to get them to college; and the final request make sure Sami has a good life. I promised I would do all three. I was concerned, I didn't know anything about raising teenage girls, but between George and I, I figured we could do it. I didn't know if we would make the right decisions, but I would give it my best shot. I didn't have a choice, and unfortunately neither did George.

By November, Barb was having good days and bad days. Sami would lay by her bed morning, noon and night. Gloria, Barb's sister, had come back up to help and to be with her sister. I was taking care of Sami on a daily basis. One day in the middle of November, Sami left Barb's side. She hadn't done this at all the whole time Barb had been sick. Now she lay at the top of the stairs. She never went into the bedroom after that. If I had to guess, I would say she knew that Barb was no longer with us; she was in her bed, but she had already left us.

On November 20, I was cleaning the house and I picked up Sami and held her so that Barb could pet Sami and Sami could say hello to her. Now for weeks, Barb didn't know either of us by name, but this particular day she opened her eyes. I said, "Barb, Sami's here." She looked at her and raised her arm to pet her, then she stretched up to tap me on my cheek and looked right at me with a smile and said, "It's okay, Mary," then closed her eyes again. I just cried. For a brief moment she remembered me and that was the very last time she spoke to me.

A few days later, my friend was gone, and Sami and her family were on their own with a little help I had hoped from me. It was a blessing and a relief, no one should ever suffer if we can help it. So I had just hoped that Barb was in a better place, and that she was healthy and smiling that sweet smile again.

On Mondays and Fridays it was my cleaning day, and the first thing I would do was take Sami for a walk, and she'd get to talk to all of her friends in the neighborhood. We could always count on Max to be at the door or outside. Max was her favorite neighborhood dog. Max was timid, but slowly got used to Sami's behavior, loud and talkative. He knew she would dance all around him and they'd say hi, and then we would be on our way. On Tuesdays and Thursdays, I would drive over at lunch and pick her up to go to Bright Eyes's house. This was Sami's very favorite time in the whole wide world. She'd be going for a car ride and a walk with Brighty, and she would just get to run and run until her heart was content. That's exactly what she would do every time. She would get out of the car and immediately start chasing birds from tree to tree around the front yard, backyard, and side yard. This girl would not stop running from the time we got there till the time we left. Bright and Sami would say hi, then Bright would want to go for a walk right away, so around the fields we would go. Short walks we would go around one field and long walks would consist of going around three fields and the cow pasture. I'd walk along the electric fence and keep telling Sami to walk on my right side. One time she failed to do so and her tail got too close to the fence. She jumped and turned immediately around to look at me, as if I did it. I just started laughing and said, "I told you to stay to my right and you didn't, so don't look at me." You could smell burnt hair. She never got close to the fence again.

I'd take her home and she'd be so tired from running. George told me she'd sleep all night. Those were the good days. Mondays and Fridays at first were hard because I had so many reminders of Barb. Often I'd find myself picking up items to dust and thinking of her, many days I'd shed tears and I would just bend over and hold Sami and instantly feel better. Then there were those days where I would cry all day while I cleaned and others I would be fine. Time is really the only healer.

The following June, Susan graduated from high school and soon was off to college. Now it was George, Beth and Sami at home. The house seemed quiet, but Beth was always playing with Sami. One time, I heard her in the other room and knew she was throwing a toy for Sami then I heard her give Sami a command "Stand." I turned my head as if I was trying to hear what she said because I must have heard her wrong. Then I heard it again, "Sami, stand!" So I walked into the room and Sami was lying there and I just looked at Beth and said, "What are you doing?" She just started laughing. "I just want to see if she will do it. She does everything else we ask her to. Sit, shake, lay down. I just wanted to see if she would stand." I just rolled my eyes and left the room laughing. I told Sami not to take that abuse. Beth just laughed and "Sami, stand" became a "standing" joke with us. Not sure Sami agreed with us about the joke.

Susan came home for the holidays, needless to say the holidays were hard, but George got the girls through them with flying colors. Always remembering, never forgetting, and soon laughter came back into the house.

Often when I would walk Sami and Brighty at Lane's, a butterfly would appear almost consistently at the same spot in the field.. It would fly in front of me, over Sami for about 30 feet then fly away. I'd say, "Sami, your mom's here looking after you." I'd watch the butterfly and say, "Hello, Barb, I am taking good care of her," and off she'd fly. I told my mom about that one time, that I'd see a butterfly and think it was Barb watching over us. She said, "That is so funny because I always thought the same thing. When I would see a butterfly I always thought it was your grandmother's way of being close to us." How many other people think this to be true? I wonder.

It's June and Beth is graduating. As I look back over the past year and a half, it is bittersweet memories for me. George and I got her through her proms and Christmas dances. George got to pay for everything and I got to shop for beautiful dresses with Beth. It was a fair trade I thought. Once again the house is filled with people and laughter. Susan is home for the summer, Gloria and Mike and some cousins are here for the graduation. Laughter and tears, but mainly laughter, and Sami loves all the attention and company that abounds.

Fall comes fast and Beth is leaving for college. That leaves George and Sami in the house. Often, I am sad because I think the two of them being lonely, but having each other, I realize, is what gets them through the days. George would visit the girls at their schools, and that meant Sami spent a lot of time with Mark and me. We loved that. Chelsea loved it. The only thing we didn't like is when it was thundering outside. Sami hated that. She would just bark in the middle of the night, thunder and fireworks set her off. That was her only downfall, if she had one at all, it was that. Her talking I could handle, but the barking in the middle of the night, I couldn't. So I would actually yell at her until she stopped. I just couldn't get her to realize she wasn't going to be hurt, and that I would protect her no matter what.

One day I decided to change the girls' sheets on their beds so they were nice and clean when they came home. The linen closet was in the hallway and all of a sudden I felt a warm feeling come over me. I smiled knowing Barb was right there with me. I just didn't know where. I slowly turned around and Sami was sitting on the step where she always sat with Barb while I'd be cleaning the bathroom. She never sat on that step before this day, so I knew Barb was sitting on her step petting Sami. I slowly turned back to the linen closet and said, "Hi, Barb. Sami is doing well and the girls are in college. All's good here." Sami came into the bedroom with me and for the first time I knew in my heart that I had accomplished what Barb had asked of me.

I often think of that day and seeing Sami on the step, I am not sure why I thought or felt she was there. I just did. It never happened again and it didn't matter. I have lost a lot of family members along the way, but often find myself thinking mostly of Barb. I can't explain that either. I know things always happen for a reason and the answer doesn't always come to us right away. Like, did I lock myself out of Abby's house that day for a reason? And was it because God knew that someday George and Barb would need me? Once again, all unanswered questions. Sometimes we get answers and sometimes we don't.

(What? You Want to Play?)

Booker

(Sittin' Pretty)

There are several times that I have met new clients from being at someone else's house. I cleaned Laura's home and across the street from her were Pat and Melissa. One day, as I was putting my cleaning supplies away in my car, Missy was putting her two kids in the car and we got to talking. She had asked me about cleaning for her and I asked her about her special dog. I often watched her dog because it was a city street, not much room to run around and he never went off the property, ever. He would watch all the school kids walk by and he never made a peep. This was my introduction to Booker, a beautiful German Shorthair Pointer.

Booker was the most obedient dog I had ever met. I often felt sorry for him as I'd watch him from across the street because I thought, here is this big graceful dog stuck on this little corner city street. He should be on a farm with a lot of property to run. I'd come to find out that Pat's family had some property and Booker often spent time with them to do exactly that. He loved going out to his grandparents' house to play and run. But as I found out later, Booker was just as happy to curl up on his bed and be around the family. He was kind and gentle with children and loving with adults. I guess you could say Booker was one in a million. He had every quality you could ever imagine a dog could ever possess. There was no leash and no fence and he still knew his boundaries, which made him the easiest dog to own. I am sure he had his moments as a puppy, but Pat must have been a terrific teacher. I remember once Missy saying that Pat had Booker before he met her, so being single he had plenty of time to train him, and he did a terrific job.

I started cleaning for Melissa and Pat and I was very happy to spend the time with Booker. I wasn't there more than two months and they found a new home. At the time they had two kids, Amanda and Jacob, and I believe Melissa was pregnant with Ali when they moved. Their new home had a larger yard for Booker and it was much larger for a growing family. Amanda and Jacob were young, and with a new baby on the way, you would think, Booker being the first one in the family, that he might be a little jealous. But he never was. He loved the kids as much as he loved Pat and Melissa. It was so uncanny that this dog was so accepting of so many changes in his life. A new house, new kids, and still loyal and loving. Like I said, the perfect dog.

I continued to clean at the new house so I never skipped a beat with Booker. He knew my car when I pulled into the driveway and he was right there at my door waiting for his treat. Missy knew when I would pull up in my car. I would bring in my cleaning supplies and he would follow me all over the house just in case I had time to pet him and pay attention to him.

Shortly after Ali was born, Melissa found herself pregnant again. Two girls and one boy and another boy on the way. The family was complete, and Booker took to the new baby in stride just as he had always done before. Nicholas would be sitting in his carrier on the floor and Booker would just come up and kiss his little face. I would look at Booker and know what he was thinking. He was so predictable, I felt I knew what he was thinking at all times. He was just that easy to read. If only kids were that easy.

I believe the first time I was dog sitting for Booker the family had gone to Florida for vacation. They always take Booker with them on vacations or he would go to Pat's parents' home, but this time they were all going to Florida, so it was my turn to stay with Booker. I couldn't wait, and I think I was more excited than Booker was. I loved this dog and I was really excited to have one-on-one time with him. I took him for car rides out to my home. We had ten acres and he loved coming out there and running. I remember my husband saying, "Now that's a dog." He loved Daisy, but he was a big dog kind of guy. We went on three or four walks a day, and we ate all our meals together. Life was good for this doggie.

Booker of course had his own big bed with his name on it. There's only the best for this dog. He'd sleep in this bed all the time, except when I was watching him. He would look at me and knew I was going to tap on the mattress and that was all he needed. He would jump up and curl up right next to me. I remember Melissa calling me and I asked her where Booker slept and she said in a strange tone, "He sleeps in his bed, why are you asking me this?" Like she knew the answer before I even said it. I said, "Well, he might be sleeping with me at night."

"No wonder he loves you so much." For seven days we were inseparable.

(Booker and me, in my paw pajamas. I think he was looking at me because I had to get up, set the camera and run back for the picture. He was probably saying, "What are you doing?")

It always surprises me how the little dogs like Daisy lay in bed with their legs out like they own the bed, and then there are my big dogs that curl into a ball and take up very little room. Well, maybe not all of them, but a majority of them do this and Booker is no exception to the rule. He never moved all night long.

Booker is my easiest dog to watch. He ate first thing in the morning, then we'd be off for our walk, he'd do his business, finish our walk and back to the house. I would have to go to work, he never seemed to mind though, because he would go lay down before I was even out of the house. He knew I would return soon enough. I would come home for lunch, we would eat and then it was time for our afternoon walk. I loved walking Booker, he wouldn't pull on his leash and he would walk right next to my side as if we were practicing for a big dog show. At night he would lay by my side, chew on his raw hide and then it was off to bed—his favorite time, not to mention, mine as well.

They had a beautiful portrait of a German Shorthair hanging in the family room. Often I'd look at it and wonder if it was Booker or one they just picked up because it looked so much like Booker. Most people will have a photo album of their pets, maybe a picture in a frame on a table, but a portrait that hangs in your family room, that's pure love.

As the kids grew, you could see the gray in Booker's face. I am not sure how old he was when I first met him, but he was now slowing down just a little bit. He would sleep more than he used to and he wasn't as agile as he once was.

It would be great if our pets lived as long as we did, then we would never have to say goodbye. Unfortunately, when that day comes it is one of the hardest things we think we are ever going to have to do. At that time, it is. But for the quality of life and because they give us all of their love their whole life, it is the one time we can truly give back. The time with Booker seemed to fly by as the years did. Pets age so quickly and we always wish we had more time with them than we do. Just as quickly as Booker came into this family's life, it seems he left just as fast. Booker was truly man's best friend, and a very large part of Pat and Melissa's family.

Not soon enough, Lilly and Leila, their two new German Shorthair puppies find their way into this fabulously warm family. And the loving continues. Booker may not be with us anymore, but he is always remembered.

Chelsea

When I came to Erie for college, I worked at the Hilton doing various jobs. I graduated from college and then began my secretarial job at the dental office. They had to hire someone to take my place and it was my job to train the new employee. The girl they chose to take my place was Ellise. She learned the cashier job really fast and she was a lot of fun to be with and to train.

A couple of years went by and I was taking my first cruise, so I called up a random travel agency and it just happened to be Ellise. She worked at the Hilton till she graduated with a degree in Travel and Tourism. I couldn't believe it had been at least four years since I had last seen her, and here she was on the other end of the phone planning my trip. Since that first trip, Ellise has been my travel agent. I had been working with her for more than ten years.

Now that I am cleaning houses, she calls me to maybe start cleaning for her. I went to her house and met her and her husband, and a beautiful friendly black Lab, Chelsea. I loved Chelsea. She was about seven years old when I first met her. She'd go outside and sit in the front yard and just watch time go by. I loved going to Ellise's because Chelsea would follow me around the house in hopes of getting a treat, which she most often did. She is our little "Honey Girl," as Ellise would always say.

Your typical black Lab, she loved going for car rides down to Grandma and Grandpa's. They had quite a bit of property so she would stay with Ellise's dad all day and follow him all over the property. She was so friendly she loved everyone, and I mean everyone; people she knew, strangers, she showed no favoritism, and never think you would be walking by the house without saying hello to her because she would come out in the street and follow you until you acknowledged her presence.

If you were willing to pet her she was willing to stay there all day and soak that attention up. Ellise and Chelsea moved to a larger home and out of the city. It was a subdivision so there were plenty of people to still say hello to. She loved her new home and her new neighbors. The house had these very large front windows that went all the way to the floor. She could lay down in the living room and still see out the windows. So while Ellise was at work that was where she stayed all day long. As soon as Ellise came home, she was back outside lying in the front yard. If you walked by with a dog, you could bet Chelsea would get up to say hello.

Her favorite dog lived across the street. His name was Alex. One might say he was her boyfriend. She would see him outside and immediately go over to see him. They would walk off in Alex's yard together and she would show up about half an hour later. I don't care if it was morning or evening, Chelsea knew when Alex was outside. He was a larger American Lab, whereas Chelsea was smaller, with that beautiful Lab face. You know the one that they put on all the rugs, pictures, and everything else that has a Lab face on it. It was easy to see why Alex liked her so much. You couldn't help it she was beautiful and her demeanor was of a typical Lab you would just love. And if you ask me, Alex loved her just as much.

I would stay with Chelsea over Easter and sometimes in April. One time Chelsea went to Virginia with us to visit my parents. She was such a good girl, she rode great and she was such an easy dog to take care of. My parents knew Chelsea from being at my house, so when I told them I was bringing her with us they were perfectly fine with that. She went on walks with us and she slept right next to my side of the bed. She didn't care who she was with, just that she was with someone. Well, I might be selling myself short, but she loved being with me, though that was my personal opinion. Along with watching her from time to time, I got to see her every other Monday, when I would clean the house, so that was our special time also.

When I watched her in April, I noticed she was having trouble going up and down the stairs. There were a lot of them and they were somewhat steep, so I would take it slowly. I did notice she was slowing down some, but at this point she had to be nine or ten years old, so it was not surprising to me that she was slower than she used to be.

When I was house-sitting her, I would walk her around several blocks, and on the days that I cleaned for Lane and Paul, she would always go with me. She loved going there. Sami was with us at every outing also. I had quite a few dogs at Lane and Paul's. They didn't mind because they all got along and they would always say, the more the merrier. She would sit outside with Brighty and she loved going on our walks together. She did it so often she knew the route by heart. She loved Chip, too. She got along with all the dogs that I had introduced her to. That made it very easy for me to take her everywhere I went. I loved my time that was spent with Chelsea, and I wanted to believe she loved spending time with me just as much.

(I was supposed to be cleaning but took time out to pet
Chelsea and Bright Eyes)

Nipper

Nipper joins our family. What a sweetie! Born March 1997 Found in a picnic shelter at WALDAMEER. Followed us everywhere.

Everyone was terribly sad that we lost PT, but remember, "When God closes a door he always leaves a window open." Here is where that saying comes into play again..

One day a black Lab puppy was left in a park pavilion. Can you imagine just dropping a dog off and leaving? Well, it couldn't have worked out any better for this puppy. It would never have found a nicer family than Steve and Nancy, and Lane and Paul for grandparents. They have Chip the beagle, aka Chipper, so they decided to name their new puppy, Nipper. He was so smart, extremely rambunctious. He learned very quickly that it was really fun to run on down the road to see Nana and Bapa where he would most certainly get treats and a great rubdown.

(Nipper smiling for the camera)

Bright Eyes was still top dog and had her spot on the couch; however, Nipper shortly wormed his way onto the couch and pawed at you to pet him. He won over Paul's heart right away. Not so much Chip's heart, but they did get along for the most part. Chip knew he was low dog on totem pole again, because of his size, but don't feel sorry for our little beagle boy. He often went out and walked the grounds, making sure all was well with nature. Every night Nancy would drive down and bring Nipper and Chipper home for bed. This became a ritual.

At Lane and Paul's, all dogs had run of the house, they could sleep and go where ever they wanted to. You could often find Chip on their bed because the windows are very big in the house and that gave him the best advantage point to the driveway to see the comings and goings. Many days I would be watching the dogs, and Brighty would be on one side of me on the couch, Nipper on the other side with Chip in the bedroom. This became the normal routine at night. Often, Bright would soon leave my side for the kitchen floor, another favorite spot of hers; however, Nipper would never leave my side. Nipper slipped into PT's spot in life very well, and soon brightened the house with his presence. I truly feel that God does have a hand in many aspects of our lives, and bringing Nipper into this family was one of them.

Nipper learned the boundaries really fast. He'd get walks every day and night and love every minute of it. Bright would stay by my side, Chip would wonder off on his own and be in the distance. I could always see him with his snoopy tail in the air and his nose to the ground. Nipper would run ahead, scope things out and run back to Bright and myself, just in case he missed something along the way.

(Bright, Nipper and Chip waiting for our walk to commence)

Nipper would get up in the morning and just have all this energy. It would last all day, then just like that he would be down and snoring. He would crash and then by the time I would go to bed, he would be the first one to run to the bedroom to get his spot on the bed. He would growl at Chip every night, and I would lift Chip on to the bed and tell Nipper to stop growling. Nipper would lay his head back down knowing I would have the final word. Bright would eventually make her way back to the bedroom and depending on the night, she would either jump on the bed or just lay on her bed. It would just depend on her mood.

These dogs were so predictable. They knew when the morning meal was being served and they would always tell me when it was 3 P.M. for their dinner. Don't worry eating dinner at 3 P.M.; it sounds early but they always had plenty of snacks in the evening. Nipper always ate his food really fast, and for some reason on this particular evening, he decided he was going to go over and finish Chip's food for him. Well, this was not okay with Chip so they started to get in a bit of a scuffle. At that moment, Bright Eyes came right over to Nipper and started fighting with Nipper. Chip backed away and I threw a pan of water on both Nipper and Bright. That was the end of that. Chip and Bright looked at me as if to say, "Hey, we didn't start that." Nipper and I would go eye-to-eye and he would know exactly where I was coming from. I opened the back door and booted them all outside to get some air. That was that. They never did that again. I went back to doing the dishes and thought to myself, "That's my girl, Brighty, looking out for the little dog." Bright Eyes received a few more kisses than normal that night.

Nipper was so easy to take care of. He was a creature of habit in every aspect of his life. He loved to chase raccoons, rabbits, and ground hogs. He was pretty fast, but not as fast as nature. I never worried about him. He was never far from my sight and would always show up five or ten minutes after we would get back from our walks. I knew that Nipper had respect for Chip because on our walks he would rely on Chip to be his hound ears and eyes. Chip would instantly perk up and do his Beagle howl. You owners of Beagles know exactly what howl I am talking about. Nipper's ears and head would perk up and he'd be thinking, "With the two of us, we can catch whatever you are on the trail of," and off he would go, pretty much with the same results—nothing. I have never seen Chip catch an animal, I think they were both in it for the chase alone.

Days ran into months, and months ran into years. Summers and winters went by quickly. Nipper loved the cold as much as he loved the heat. The bigger dogs liked the winters the most. Nipper and Bright would sit out in the front of the house in the snow for hours just taking in the daylight. Nipper would often sit on a snow bank and pretend to be king of the hill. Many times on our winter walks, little snowballs would form on the pads of the dog's feet. Bright would just stop walking, sit down and start chewing the snow from the bottom of her feet. Sometimes she would just sit there and look at me until I came over and pulled the snow from her pads, then we would continue on with our walk. Nipper wouldn't stop, being too afraid of missing something. He would look at me as if to say, "Hey, could you get these things off of me so I can continue on with my walk?" In the thicker snow this happened quite frequently as we made our way around the fields, then we would get to the driveway and no more snowballs would appear on their feet.

(Sometimes Chip & Nipper were best friends.)

(Bright and Nipper in the snowy background. These two were inseparable)

In the hot summer months, Nipper loved going down to the lake and spending time with the family. I gave Bright an orange doggy life vest, but since Bright Eyes didn't go on the boat anymore, they let Nipper use it. So they would put the vest on Nipper and he would swim out to the boat to be with the family and to cool down. He loved just being with Paul on his boat. He loved being with Paul wherever he was.

(Nipper at his favorite summer pastime)

Nipper was happiest when he was around the family, kids, grandparents, anyone. Everyday Nipper would wake up and make his way down to Paul and Lane's where he would spend every minute of the day and night. Nancy had a big bed for Nipper and a little round bed for Chip. Many times, if Chip got to the big bed first, that was where he stayed for the night and then Nipper cuddled up in a little ball and squeezed himself into Chip's bed. Nipper didn't even seem to mind and sometimes he preferred it. I loved watching Nipper squeeze into Chips bed.. I bought Chip a little round bed for Lane's house so he would have a bed down there to lie on and he used it a lot, but at home he always chose the big bed to lie in.

(Chip on Nipper's bed and Nipper curled up in Chip's bed)

One day I got a call from Lane. Nipper had collapsed in the orchard and wasn't moving. They ran him into their veterinary hospital where he spent four days. He was so sick, and they diagnosed him with severe pancreatitis. We were all trying to figure out what he could have gotten into. The only thing we could surmise was an animal that may have been sick already, or maybe an animal that was already dead that he somehow got a hold of. He was not getting any better so they referred him to Orchard Park Veterinary Hospital in Buffalo. It was two hours away but they were the best, so there was no hesitation to take Nipper there. After the same diagnosis that the Erie hospital came up with, the outcome was dim at best. Nipper was so sick. The family listened to the doctors and then discussed the treatment and they made the final decision to do whatever it took to get Nipper healthy again. He was so sick they didn't even put him in a cage. He was lying on blankets outside of the cages hooked up to IV's and machines to monitor his vitals. They had to operate but because he was so sick, they knew he wouldn't make it through surgery, so they had to get him healthy enough where he had a chance to make it through surgery.

Paul was so upset he called a family meeting and said that there couldn't be a day where Nipper was alone, so he set up a schedule that someone in the family would be with him every day. Lane and Paul had Sundays and Wednesdays. Nancy and Steve had Mondays, Fridays and Saturdays, and I had Tuesdays and Thursdays.

They were so good at the hospital. We would get there, tell them we were there, and within five minutes we were being escorted back to where Nipper lay. This went on for three solid weeks. It was the best veterinary hospital I had ever been to. They were so caring and you could just tell they loved all the animals. I thought they went above and beyond with Nipper, but as I watched them work in the treatment room on all the other animals, they were over and above with every animal that came through those doors.

I knew Nipper was in great hands with these doctors. In three weeks, the improvement was very slow. Nipper would know when we were there. He'd perk up whenever he saw one of us. Dr. Brummer felt our visits were good for Nipper and felt in order for him to pull through, he needed to see us. So it was very important for us to keep up the schedule that we had to get him through this. We all loved Nipper very much. Working at a veterinary hospital, I had seen a lot of very sick animals, and yet Nipper was the sickest dog I had ever seen. It broke our hearts to see him like this. Whoever was with him that day would come home and call everybody to give us an update from their visit. The report was always the same, no improvement but happy to see us. Dr. Brummer never gave us false hope. They were always up front and we knew what we were dealing with at all times. You could only imagine what clinical care cost, so they would update Nancy and Steve with the financials because you never know. Most people wouldn't put this much money into an animal, but again when discussed with the family, there wasn't any question, we do what is necessary. That's why I say that any animal that is rescued by this family is the luckiest animal on earth.

Orchard Park Hospital was truly the best in its field. The doctors would take the time to talk to each and everyone that visited with Nipper, and you could tell they loved Nipper very much, the whole staff from the doctors to the technicians. You could just feel it when you were there. Even though we would be with Nipper on the floor, they would come over every now and then and see if we needed anything. After three weeks, Dr. Brummer said if he was going to do the surgery this was the time. He felt Nipper wasn't going to get any better without the surgery so it was imperative that we do the surgery. He had improved from where he was when he first got there, but without the surgery he wasn't going to get better. Not once getting our hopes up, but encouraging us enough to get through this ordeal.

The surgery was set for Wednesday afternoon. Our thoughts were on nothing but Nipper this day. I held my breath until the time I would get a phone call. I was cleaning Booker's house when the call came in at 2 P.M. Nipper was out of surgery, he made it through and was in the recovery room. He still wasn't out of the woods, but it was hopeful that he even made it through the surgery. I had a sigh of relief and thanked God for his help. I was cleaning the downstairs bathroom and received another call about half an hour later. Nipper passed away going from the recovery room to his bed. I just sobbed. This dog, as well as the doctors, gave it their all but it was just too much for him to endure. I then asked God to watch over our beloved animal.

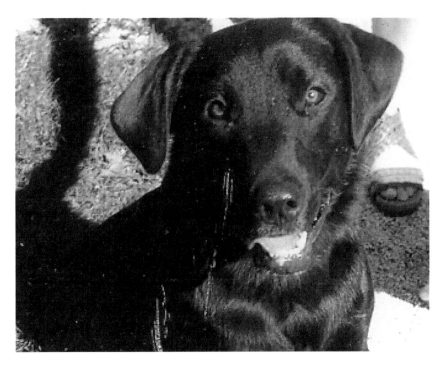

(Just Pet Me!)

I can't say enough about the care Nipper received from the Orchard Park Veterinary Hospital. There wasn't anything they didn't do for him or that they couldn't do. That was the best treatment an animal could have ever received. A few days after Nipper passed, Nancy and Steve received a nice letter from Orchard Park. They said how sorry they were that he hadn't made it and how much the staff loved Nipper. One day when Nancy was talking to Dr. Brummer, she asked him what he believed happens to a pet when they pass away, this was what he said they all believe:

Rainbow Bridge

Just this side of Heaven is a place called Rainbow Bridge. When an animal dies that has been especially close to someone here, that pet goes to Rainbow Bridge. There are meadows and hills for all our special friends, so they can run and play together. There is plenty of food, water, and sunshine, and our friends are warm and comfortable. All the animals that had been ill and old are restored to health and vigor, those who were hurt or maimed are made whole again. Just remember them in our dreams of days and times gone by.

The animals are happy and content, except for one small thing: They each miss someone very special to them, who had to be left behind. They all run and play to-

gether, but the day comes when one suddenly stops and looks into the distance. His bright eyes are intent, his eager body begins to quiver. Suddenly he begins to run from the group, flying over the green grass, his legs carrying him faster and faster. You have been spotted and when you and your special friend finally meet, you cling together in joyous reunion, never to be parted again.

The happy kisses rain upon your face, your hands again caress the beloved head and you look once more into the trusting eyes of your pet. So long gone from your life, but never absent from your heart. Then you cross the Rainbow Bridge together....
Author Unknown

For some odd reason, this is what got us through the sadness. Knowing that Nipper was his playful self once again and picturing him running in fields and laying in the sun again helped us all. Still so terribly missed but somehow comforted that one day we will see Nipper again.

(Nipper's favorite time, sitting with Brighty and Paul in the sun)

Sami

(Sami posing in front of forsythia bush, notice tennis ball in front of her)

Two years have now passed. The girls are solid in college and George has decided it's time to move, which means my time with Sami—and let me tell you, it has been a lot of time—is coming to an end. I knew it would be a while before the house is sold and everything is final, but it will still come too soon and I am going to cherish every minute that I have left with her. The house sold really fast. George was really surprised, but I wasn't.

I was the cleaning lady, and I knew it would go fast. (Yes, I am tooting my own horn. I am allowed. I'm the writer.) The girls came home for the summer. They were sad it was their last summer in the home they grew up in. We had a lot of packing and deciding what would stay and what would go. George couldn't believe all the stuff they had collected over the years. The girls had fun remembering all the play horses and stables they had, once again the house was filled with laughter and tears. They knew it was the best thing for all of them. The girls were going to go their own ways after college, and George needed a change of scenery. It was best for everyone, except Sami and me. George had asked me one more favor. Would I please take Sami for a month while he moves and gets settled? Umm, let me think about that. Hell, yeah, I would take her for the month. She was as much my dog as she was his. Our time together was precious. We continued our walks and trips to Brighty's home. She went everywhere with me.

(Sami in a messy bedroom)

(Don't judge my cleaning by this picture, the girls' rooms were all theirs to clean when they came home, and Sami I thought for sure would get lost in Beth's room so I took a picture to prove she was in the room somewhere)

Beth called me and said she was coming up. She visited her friends and spent Saturday night with Mark and me. Sami slept in our bed with us. Sunday afternoon and it was time to let her go. Sad day for me but I knew I would see Sami again. She was happy to be going for a ride and she was with Beth. Life was good. As I watched them drive off, I noticed smiles on both their faces, as tears streamed down mine.

Two years go by again and we receive an invitation in the mail to Beth's college graduation. Where does the time go? The family was meeting in Virginia for the weekend. George rented a very large condo and when we got there, George and Susan and Beth were there along with Gloria and Mike. We were all there laughing and joking having dinner together again. George didn't bring Sami. He thought we would be too busy and wasn't sure how she would do in the condo. Sami was at home with her new dog sitter, which I was told she loved just as much as me (impossible), but I felt good that she had someone new in her life that loved her just as much as I did. I was disappointed but I understood.

Graduation was great and then we all went out for dinner to celebrate. It was an absolutely great time. A lot of laughter, food, and of course, several bottles of wine and champagne were had by all. Once again it was time to say goodbye to everyone and when we left we said we would see them all soon. Mark and I are planning a trip to George's to spend time with Sami and the family.

My walks still continue with Bright Eyes and guess what is missing—our butterfly. I have not seen it since Sami stopped walking with us. I can only assume that Barb is with Sami, and that thought warms my heart.

(Sami with her favorite toy, the tennis ball.)

Bogey and Babe

(Bogey sitting pretty for the camera)

My phone rang and I didn't recognize the number, and I didn't even recognize the voice even though I knew I should. It was Chris from the dental office of where I used to work.. Her and her husband Brian were going on a vacation and they had heard that I dog sit. Her mother usually watched the dogs, but this particular time her mom was going with them on the trip. Lucky for me. I set up a time to meet with the dogs and I was greeted by two big dogs. We hit it off right away. Bogey was a beautiful Akita mix and Babe was a mixed black Lab. She had very big ears like a German Shepherds, but I was not sure what she was actually mixed with. What I do know was she was very, very sweet. I was looking forward to my time with my two new dogs.

It was in March so it was still pretty snowy on the ground. I wasn't sure how they would greet me my first time coming in alone, so I talked to them as soon as I walked in the door, with a very calm voice. I didn't need to; they were both very excited to see me and talked to me as soon as I came in. Chris had explained the regiment to me and it was clear right from the start they knew it to be gospel. They went out as soon as I came in. They had fence in the yard so they didn't get walks, though they just liked being outside. Bogey liked the outdoors more so than Babe. I called her Baby because she was just that, my little baby. Bogey was like that little ten-year-old boy you loved but knew you had to watch at all times. He was so mischievous, not bad, and just tried to get away with a lot more than he should. He wasn't allowed on the couch and yet that was the first place he would be when I came home from work. I would just look at him and say, "What are you doing? Are you on the couch?" and off he would jump. He had such a bear-like face you just wanted to squeeze it because he was so stinking cute.

(Bogey outside in the snow, his favorite place to be)

(Babe doing what she loves, lying in living room with the family)

I was knitting scarves at the time and Baby would sit at my side the whole night. Bogey would inevitably end up on the couch by 10 P.M., but don't tell Chris and Brian that. Bedtime was just great. They would race up the stairs and jump right on their bed. They had a blanket on the bed and that was where they both slept through the night. I slept in the guest bedroom. I would brush my teeth and check on them as if to tuck them in for the night, and they would be lying there with their eyes almost shut. Bedtime was their favorite time. Wait, I take that back: morning was their favorite time. I didn't need an alarm, for they were both in my room by 7 A.M. jumping on the bed and wanting to go out. They would eat their breakfast and then be back outside. Baby would go out and come right back in, but Bogey would be outside the whole morning. He has that beautiful thick coat where he just loves the cold air.

In the spring in this area, our backyards are like swamps from all the snow that has melted. Babe likes to go out run around and back in to sit with me. Bogey on the other hand will stay outside for hours and with his white paws, they would get so muddy he no longer had white paws but black paws. I had to dip his paws in warm water before he could even think of coming in the house. He didn't seem to mind this; however, and the water was just thick with mud when we were done. He liked to get brushed, and believe me, his coat was so thick with undercoat that the only time I would brush him was when he was outside. Other than that, I would be sweeping and filling up a whole vacuum bag with hair. So I used the shedding brush on him and I could make another dog with all the hair I would get off him. He would look at me as if to say, "I'll give you an hour to stop that." He just stood there and let me brush, brush, brush him. He has such a fabulous beautiful coat. He shined when he was done.

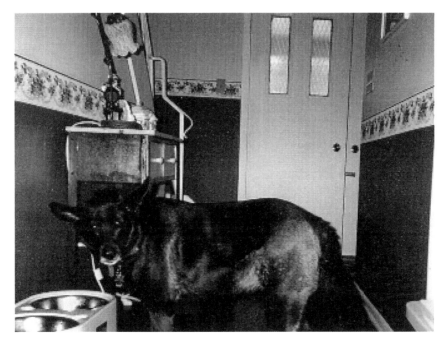

(Eating, my next favorite hobby)

I enjoyed my time with Bogey and Baby because they were so easy to sit. They were so excited when I came home from work every day, and they made coming home a very happy occasion. I only watched them a few times because Chris's mom watches them mostly. I miss them, but I see Christine at bowling and she tells me they are doing just fine. They built a new home a couple years ago and I guess Bogey had a hard time getting used to the new house, but he is doing just fine now.

When I was remembering Bogey and Babe, I said to Christine, "I am finishing up with Bogey and Babe, but I can't remember, is it Babe or Baby?" She just laughed. She said, "It was Babe, but since you watched them and called her Baby, we call her Baby now. It stuck with her." I just laughed. I changed their dog's name and didn't even know it. I just smile when I think of these two dogs. I hope to see and stay with them again, but I understand why mom gets them usually.

When I completed this book, I sent out consent forms to make sure everyone had known that I was writing about them and their dogs. When I received Christine's consent form back in the mail, it was signed and attached was a note: "Mary, good luck with the book. We lost Babe last August, so I hope she will still be mentioned. Chris." My eyes welled up with tears as I read this note and my thoughts went straight to Babe. I have several animals up at "Rainbow Bridge" and asked them to watch over Babe for me till someone came for her. Babe will be sadly missed, I suspect mostly by Bogey. All my love goes out to the family and to Babe.

Heidi

(Heidi striking a pose for the camera)

After Nipper died, Nancy and Steve just felt they were ready for another dog. They had Chip but Nancy liked having two dogs. She thought she would like a "Sami" dog, a Sheltie. She liked that size and thought it would be good for Chip to have a talkative dog to hang with. She had asked me about a Bichon, but I didn't think it's a good dog for her. They have so much property for the dogs to run on and a white fluffy dog just didn't fit in the picture. They need a lot of grooming and they just don't have the time that a Bichon requires. It's important to find the right dog for your lifestyle and family style.

Weeks went by and Emily said she wanted a smaller dog that fits in her lap. The rest of the family really didn't care. They just knew they wanted a puppy to fill the void of Nipper. I just told her to take her time and see where things go. Something would come to them eventually.

Low and behold, a puppy was being given away by someone Nancy knew. The owner said, they were going to get rid of her because she was unteachable, didn't listen, and she wasn't very smart and they were just going to have her put down. That was all Nancy needed to hear—put down because she wasn't very smart. Are you kidding me? Come on, people, think about it. If we put down children because of every time they didn't listen to us, the population would be null and void. I don't believe in not very smart dogs, just not smart people, but enough about that. Nancy felt sorry for this puppy and since they were looking for a new dog, the family received a new black puppy, and they named her Heidi.

I went to work on Wednesday and it was my first day meeting Heidi. I walked into the kitchen and this little black dog just started jumping on me all excitedly. I looked at Heidi and then looked at Nancy. I said hello to Heidi then said to Nancy, "Nancy, have you seen this puppy's paws?" She just started laughing. I said, "What happened to a smaller dog, a lap dog?" She said to me, "Sometimes we don't get to pick our dogs, they pick us." How true that statement is. I don't think I have had a puppy in over twenty years because all my dogs are older rescue dogs. I loved Nancy's answer, and I loved this new puppy. I could tell she was going to be handful.

Let me explain why I was just a little surprised when meeting Heidi for the first time. She was about three months old and she had these HUGE paws. She had this square head that was way too big for her body. If you have ever seen Turner and Hooch, she was going to be Hooch. She looked just like Hooch's offspring. Remember that puppy in the closet when Tom Hanks was going over the rules one more time? Well, that was exactly what Heidi looked like. She was a Pit Bull, Rottweiler mix. She was going to be huge. Not quite the lap dog that Emily wanted (Don't tell Heidi that) although she believes she is a lap dog. She was the perfect dog for an out-of-the-way home with no neighbors and a lot of land to run. She will be the protector of the house just as soon as she grows into her head and her paws.

The first time I watched Heidi, I also had the kids and Brighty and Chip to watch as well. Heidi loved Bright because she would play with her, and Bright Eyes was very gentle with her, always the mother hen. She would play with her for only so long then Bright would let Heidi know enough was enough. Heidi wanted to play 24/7. Bright had to be close to eight years old, so her playing time was limited. Eventually, Heidi learned the rules. She knew Bright was alpha dog, and when they played, Bright would put Heidi's whole head in her mouth, as Heidi was always trying to bite Bright's legs. They loved to play together. Bright was definitely the mom in the group, knowing she was a puppy and had to play, but letting Heidi know when she was done playing, then Heidi would leave her alone and move on to the next toy.

When the dogs are at Nancy's, they all have their own beds in the kitchen. Chip often slept on Brighty's bed with her. Heidi had her own large bed for her growing body. Don't get me wrong, Chip had his own bed but always slept on the bigger beds. He's another one of my little dogs with a big dog mentality. They were all so cute when they were laying on their beds. The kids spent most of their time in the kitchen doing homework or crafts so that's where the dogs hung out as well.

(Bright and Chip always shared a bed…)

All the dogs that Lane and Paul and Nancy and Steve have had walked without leashes and they stayed in the confines of the property, except Heidi. Heidi would run off whenever she could. She wasn't stupid or untrainable like the previous owner thought; she was just a puppy. They took her to obedience school as soon as she was old enough to go. She was such a large dog, so they wanted her to know her limits and they wanted her to listen to them. She was still jumping on people when they entered the house, and Nancy didn't want her to do this. It was like having a bear jump on you with nails digging into your shoulders. It didn't matter how much they corrected her–this was one thing she was not going to stop doing.

As I said before, Heidi was a Pit Bull, Rottweiler mix. For anyone who has Pit Bulls you know two things: They are headstrong, and I don't mean because their heads are so big, and they tend to do whatever they want. Thus, the obedience classes are a must when training these dogs. They weren't working very well as Nancy had hoped. Heidi still had to be walked on a leash because she just wouldn't stay with her on their walks, and on a leash it literally felt like she was ripping out your arm because she was pulling so hard for wanting to run. She was still jumping on people to say hello when they entered the house. Puppies are hard to train. Because of her size it was frustrating for Nancy, but it was just something they needed to stay with. They knew some things were not going to change and others would with age. Time would tell what she would learn and not learn. She was not a stupid dog; she was a very loving dog. She would stay, sit, come and shake, but she would always jump with excitement. Take the good with the bad. I loved it when she would jump on me, so I wasn't good to have around. I would make her jump on me and then we would dance around the kitchen floor. She loved it and I loved it, but Nancy did not. If you know anything about me, you know that I don't really care about what the owners want or don't want. The dogs and I have a bond that we don't break. I let Heidi jump on me and Nancy just shakes her head and laughs.

Steve and Nancy decided to put in an invisible fence so that Heidi could run free in the yard. She had a lot of space to run and this was just fine with Heidi. She learned very quickly what the boundaries were and she abided by them always and still to this day. There was plenty of room to exhaust herself, which she did on a daily basis, and she was out of harm's way of running away and getting lost. Her favorite toy for outside is a basketball. She ruins them all but she loves running and playing with them. She will play soccer with them and she will put them in her mouth and run around the yard, and she likes it best when you chase her. She was getting so big and so strong. She nearly knocks me over when she sees me.

Heidi still jumps on my chest and she still gets yelled at, but some things will never change. I just don't see Nancy winning this battle. I am not sure if she jumps on everybody or just me. If it is just me, that's okay, but if it's everybody, she'll have to learn.

It's Christmas and I have all three dogs. Chip stays out of the way of Heidi and Bright. He does try sometimes to get involved with their play time, then gives up when he realizes he isn't going to get anywhere with them. Heidi and Bright just continue on. When Bright Eyes had enough, she will stand at the back door so she can go out and lie in the snow. Heidi runs out in front of her and continues on with their playing outside.

Christmas morning and it's time to open their gifts from Santa. Bright gets a new nylabone that she instantly takes outside and begins to chew. I said to her, "You don't even want to see what Chip and Heidi get from Santa?" She stands at the back door until I open it, and out she goes. Heidi gets new doggie dishes with a stand so her food is at her height, plus a new bone. Outside she goes. Chip gets a couple of new toys and starts to chew on them right away. After I cook up some scrambled eggs and bacon, we head off for our morning walk. After that it's time to watch a movie and let the dogs nap. It was a good Christmas for all of us.

(Chelsea and Heidi partying with the rest of us on New Year)

Bright loves her time with Heidi, but she likes the breaks she gets when Lane and Paul come home. Heidi just likes everything. She curls into this little ball when she sleeps, and often times when I come downstairs in the morning, she is curled up in Chip's little bed, her head hanging over the side and then Chip is sprawled out on Heidi's big bed. It just makes me laugh. It reminds me once again of Nipper.

I saw Chip and Heidi every Wednesday, and each time I was greeted with such enthusiasm. Heidi would jump on me as usual. Chip would wait till Heidi was finished and then come over to say hi, the proper way, with a big Beagle howl. I would make three trips in and out bringing in my cleaning supplies, and immediately Heidi would come out with me and run right to her basketball so I could play outside with her. This would go on for about 20 minutes, then when I was cleaning the house, she would come and sit in front of me and I knew she wanted me to pet her. Who am I to argue? She's a big dog.

In November, I had the kids and the dogs. The kids were all in bed by 9:30 so that left an hour or so for the dogs. Chip was sleeping in his bed, but Heidi would be in the living room with me. She sits in front of me and demands that I pet her. I really mean demanding. She sits and stares at you then her paw comes up and lets you know in no uncertain terms, you will be petting her. As soon as you touch her, she scoots around so her back is getting the rub down. This was pretty much the normal around here. I had to make sure the kids were up for school, which they were great about, and then the dogs and I were off for our morning walk. Heidi on her leash, Bright walking right next to me, and Chip nearby in the field never out of sight. The week always goes by so fast when I am watching the dogs and the kids. The kids have such busy schedules and the dogs keep me busy at home, and before I know it I was saying goodbye again. This was always my best week, when I had the kids and the dogs together.

A few short weeks and I am back at Steve and Nancy's, except it's only the dogs this time—Bright, Chip and Heidi. All the dogs sleep in the kitchen. I don't like that because my bedroom is so far away from them. I never know if any of them will need me during the night. Chip sometimes has accidents so he has to stay in the kitchen, but Bright and Heidi come and get in bed with me. Don't tell Nancy. It makes me feel better knowing they are right by my side.

(Heidi and Bright just waiting for something to drop on the floor)

When we go for our daily walks, Heidi is still in training, so the rule is when she pulls, you tell her to stop. You stop walking so she understands what stop means. If it's so bad that you can't stop her, you are supposed to drop the leash. One Saturday night we were out on our evening walk at around 5 P.M., dusk and feeding time for the deer. Chip was up ahead and decided to chase them down.. Heidi was on the leash tugging my arm out of its socket and Bright was next to me. I let go of the leash so she would stop, but instead Heidi took off after Chip. She would stop when she got to the tree line. Bright stayed right at my side and I went right to the spot where Chip and Heidi went in and I didn't see them anywhere. I was mad at myself because I didn't consider Chip being in front of Heidi when I let the leash go. Chip was a runner and as long as someone was following him, he'd just keep going. The only problem with that was Chip knew these woods inside and out, and he knew his way home. Heidi could stay with Chip but she's on a leash, so she could get tangled up easily.

I kept calling her name but to no avail. I walked Bright up to the house and put her inside. I wasn't worried yet because I thought Chip would turn back and come to the house. I went out and walked back down the tree line of the woods. I'd call out their names, but nothing. I couldn't even hear any barking. I walked my way back to the house and called my husband, Rick. He said he'd come down and walk the woods with me. I now started to worry so I decided to get in my car and drive down the driveway to the main road and see if I could hear or see them.

I was elated. As I was driving down the road, Chip was walking down the road towards me. I pulled over and he just came up the car like it was nothing and got in. I was talking to him as if I would get an answer, "Chip, where is Heidi? Point me in the direction you went, where did you just come from?" I didn't get anything from him. I rolled down my window and was calling Heidi's name, but nothing. It was getting darker and darker. I took Chip home so I didn't have to worry about him as well.

In the meantime, Rick showed up. He was a hunter so he was ready to get into the woods, thinking of course that Heidi wasn't coming out because she was probably wrapped around a tree by her leash. We walked the back woods together. We saw turkeys and more deer, but no sign of Heidi. At this point I was extremely worried, and all these bad thoughts were going through my head. Did someone pick her up and would they just take her? She's such a big girl, would they use her for dog fights? Then I just went into panic mode.

I decided I had to call Nancy and Steve and tell them. When I got a hold of them, Paul immediately got on the phone and called the grounds keepers to come over and help scan the woods. I wasn't sure if I should call and worry them or ruin their trip. The response I received was, "Absolutely, you call, we can always pray for you and give you any advice or help as much as possible." So I hung up the phone and started to cry. The grounds keepers showed up, and Rick and I told them where we had been and they started on the neighbors' woods and walked back to where we had stopped. They started at one end and we started at the other and we met in the middle of the woods, but once again, nothing. Where was she? We were convinced she was not in those woods. Rick went home and Chuck and Chuck Jr. fed the cows and left.

At this point, it was dark and the temperature was dropping to 38 degrees for the evening. I was sick. I hadn't seen either hide or hair of Heidi, and I didn't know what to do next. I was pretty cold so I took a hot bath. As I sat in the tub, I just sobbed like I have never cried before. I couldn't even catch my breath. I felt guilty sitting in a hot tub when Heidi was somewhere outside. I hoped she was outside and not with someone else. I hoped someone didn't pick her up and take her. I just had that pit in my stomach of helplessness. Whatever made me think I was qualified to take care of other people's animals? I was just cursing myself and doubting my abilities even though I had been doing this for years.

I got out of the tub and my eyes were so swollen from crying. Nancy called and asked if I had any luck, but I didn't have good news for her. I decided to grab my pillow and blanket and sleep on the kitchen floor with Bright and Chip. If Heidi came to the back door I wanted to hear her. Brighty could tell something was wrong and Chip could care less. It was life as usual for him.

Morning came and no one came barking at the door. I got up, dressed, and fed the dogs then I found pictures of Heidi and went and copied them on my computer. By 8 A.M., I was distributing them to any place of business that was close to the area. I placed them on poles at the corners of neighboring streets. I got back to the house at 10:30 and decided I would start walking the woods again. I was so sad. I didn't hear any howling or barking or whining. Chuck Jr. was there and was combing the area again. I decided to go over to the subdivision and start knocking on doors, house to house, but most people hadn't seen her. Everyone felt bad and wished me luck. I can only imagine what my face looked like as I told my sad story. One man said he did see her, but because she was so big he didn't want to approach her. He wasn't sure of her temperament. My heart skipped a beat. At last a small sign of hope, very small. "Do you have any idea which way I should go or which way she headed off last?" He told me to check the houses behind him, and he said the woods there are pretty thick, so she could be there. I drove around and these houses were all posted with private driveways. I called Rick and told him where I was and about the private driveway signs, and he told me to just go ahead, and if anyone questioned me, he told me to tell them why I was there.

I pulled into a driveway and started walking into the woods in the direction of where the gentleman told me to go. I went as far as I could one way because the brush was so thick with thorns. I was calling her name the whole way and seeing nothing. Where I had a glimmer of hope that maybe someone had seen her was slowly fading away. I slowly walked backwards and went in another direction. I couldn't get far because it was just so thick, and I thought how she could ever get through this if she was back here. With a heavy sigh I started back to my car. Then I heard what I thought was a little whimper, maybe a noise that just came out of my own mouth. Was it a little bird making that noise, maybe a chipmunk? I turned around again and called out Heidi's name. The little noise had come from the first direction I had gone in. Listening ever so hard, I didn't hear anything and I thought my ears were playing tricks on me. I started to go in that first direction again calling out her name, "Heidi! Heidi!"

Then there it was, just a little moan, ever so slightly, I could barely make it out. As I walked to exactly where I had been standing just minutes before, there she was just sitting up straight like a statue looking at me as if to say, "I can't move and if I am in trouble I don't want to say a word." I yelled, cried and held her like she's never been held before. She was all tangled with her leash in the thick thorny brush. I couldn't get her free from the bushes so I just unhooked her leash and she ran right to my car. I turned at the spot where I had just found her and I must have been standing right by her side the first time. That was how silent and unmovable she was. She never made a peep or a move until she saw me walking away. I actually didn't think about that till later. I ran back to my car and cried and hugged her. On my way home, I called Rick and just yelled into the phone, "I found her, I found her." I was just crying and every emotion I could possibly think of was coming over me at that moment. I was exhausted and elated, and I couldn't wait to tell Steve and Nancy, the kids, and Paul and Lane that I had found her. I couldn't touch her enough. Rick was very happy for me and Heidi, and he said, "You are tenacious, and if I am ever lost in the woods, I want you to lead the search party."

When I got back to the house, Chuck and Chuck Jr. were there in the barn and she ran over to them to give them a great big hello. They were very happy to see her. I called Nancy's cell, but because they were in the air, the phones were turned off. I just couldn't wait to talk to them. Bright immediately came up to her and said, "Where did you go? Mary was sick about you. Don't do that again." Heidi went straight to her bed and started to sleep. She was pretty cold. I checked her out and she had some cuts from the thorns on her belly, but that was about it. So I treated her cuts, covered her with a blanket, and off to never never land she went. She was exhausted too. I was relieved.

I went upstairs and took another hot bath, but this time I sat in the tub and cried with joy and thanked God over and over again. The day before had been the worst day of my life and today just couldn't get any better.

It was now 2:30 and I was just watching the clock. I didn't know if the family would call or not or what time they would be touching down, so I watched and I waited. The phone rang and I ran to it. It was Nancy. Paul didn't want her to call; he just couldn't take any more bad news. They had just touched down in the Pittsburgh airport and she just had to call. Then I just started yelling, "I found her, she's home." Then she yelled it out in the airport and all I could hear in the background was jubilation. "She found her, she's home. Heidi is home." Everyone was so happy their dog was home and their vacation ended on a happy note. Nancy was so glad she called, although she wasn't going to, but she had to know. They couldn't wait to get home.

Lane wanted me to show her where she was stuck and Paul said absolutely not and he didn't want to know. He was just glad and thankful I found her. Heidi has never tried to run away ever again.

I get to see her every other Tuesday, and it is always with a big jump on my chest. Some things never change, but since the day I found her we have had a special bond. She knows it and I know it. I watch her every Christmas still, and no, I have never let the leash go again. She can drag me with her, but I am never letting go of the leash ever again. She is a couple years older now and she has since stopped pulling on the leash, no longer ripping my arm out of the socket, and when she sees a deer she just stands there and watches it. She doesn't try to chase it anymore. I think she learned her lesson, as did I.

I have often thought of that day and why or how she didn't make a peep when I had to be standing right next to her. Any other dog would have been barking or making some kind of noise of excitement seeing me standing there.

But a few years have passed and it is still the same. When Heidi is caught behind a door or caught somewhere where she is stuck, she just sits there. She doesn't make a sound. It strikes me so funny because it's just not what a dog would ever do. It's not a good thing because I never know when she is in distress or in need of help. It is scary. The only thing Lane and I can think of is, maybe as a puppy she would get in trouble if she made any noise, so it's maybe a learned behavior. Other than that, we don't have any other explanation for it. Therefore, I am constantly checking on her, and whenever I spend the night, she doesn't sleep in the kitchen—she is right next to me in bed where I can keep an eye on her at all times.

To this day I get greeted every time I go in the house with an inevitable amount of love. Chip even knows that Heidi always greets first then Chip comes over to say hello. Once I was out in the yard and Heidi just ran at full speed to me. I made the mistake of bending over and our heads collided. I literally was knocked off my feet and knocked out silly for a few minutes. Nancy came out running to see if I was okay. I was, I just got up and shook my head like a cartoon character. That's love. Even though when you come to the house your first reaction is to say to yourself, "Whoa, back away slowly," until you get to know her and then you say to yourself, "Is she for sale?" It's not just me, it's everyone. The UPS drivers love her. The chimney sweepers and anyone who is doing painting or any maintenance on the house, they all want to steal her, and anyone who knows her thinks she is the best. Needless to say, the small puppy that was stupid and couldn't learn a thing is the one dog that everyone wishes they had. Sweet, sweet, Heidi. The most loving and adorable dog ever. Did I say fast? Very fast dog ever.

(Heidi and Jimmy on New Year's Eve, and yes, she really is this sweet)

Burbank

(The day we brought Burbank home, Rick and Burbank)

Burbank is probably my luckiest unlucky dog ever. I found him or should I say he found us when we lived in a small community. One Saturday morning, my trip to the bank was somewhat disturbing. I pulled up to the drive thru and a hairy black dog jumped on my car. It scared the daylights out of me. I asked the teller where this dog came from. She said it had been there for three days now. I petted it and drove out of the bank parking lot. I went home and told my husband about this dog. I felt terrible because that had meant that it probably hadn't eaten anything in three days or more. All day long my mind wondered back to the bank.

We drove past the bank that night to go bowling and there he was lying under the teller window. It wasn't cold, but it had started raining. When we drove past the bank on our way home, we didn't see the dog that night. It was raining pretty hard and I decided that in the morning I would go back to the bank and bring the dog home if he was still there.

Morning couldn't come fast enough for me. I drove around the drive thru and sure enough the dog was still there. I opened the car door and the dog jumped in like it was mine since birth. Friendly didn't describe this dog. I pulled into the garage and he wanted to go in the house right away. I first had to check the dog over. He was a she. She was all black. She had the face and hair of a Golden Retriever and just a little smaller than Bright Eyes. I got a bowl of food and water for her. Not too much because I knew she would gobble it down like there was no tomorrow. She was happy. I called Lisa about getting her groomed and cleaned up for me. She said she didn't want to bring her to her place not knowing whether she had her vaccines, but that she would come to my house and we could clean her up right away.

She loved the attention she was getting. Lisa said she was a matted mess. She was very good about getting brushed out though. She didn't like it but she didn't give us any problems. She was full of burrs head to toe. She was brushed out and then she got her bath outside. She looked like a different dog when Lisa was finished with her. I had a doggy bed for her and I didn't want her in the house till I had taken her to the vet. First thing Monday morning, I would call for an appointment.

She would stand by the back door in the garage just wanting to come in. I don't know how long she had been on the run, but she was dirty enough that it could have been a very long time. I turned on the radio for her so she wouldn't be lonely and she finally settled in for the night. I was sure it was a long day for her, maybe much longer than I could have ever imagined. As I watched her to make sure she did calm down, I thought of what I would call her. It didn't take me long to come up with her name. She was full of burrs and I found her at the bank–Burbank.

I couldn't get her into the vet till Thursday, so she had a few more days in the garage. There was so much dirt on her when she got her bath, and Lisa said it was hard to tell if she had fleas or not, so I didn't want to take a chance and bring them into the house. She would have to wait till I could get her on flea prevention medicine before I would bring her in. As the days went by, I couldn't believe how adapted she had become to us. She would follow us all around the yard. I was worried at first if she would take off again if given the chance. My question was soon answered; this dog was going nowhere. We couldn't move without her being at our heels. Rick decided he would take her for a walk in our woods behind the house. We found out what her favorite plaything was. Water. He took her down to the creek and she didn't hesitate. She went right into the water and started swimming around. He must have been gone for an hour. I thought surely she had run off and he was trying to find her. Nope, not the case. He had been throwing sticks in the water and she was fetching them. He couldn't get her out of the water. But as soon as he started walking away she was right by his side. I am telling you, it was like she was ours from the start. Not that I was happy that she smelled like a creek just after Lisa and I spent hours cleaning her up, but whatever made her happy was alright with me.

(Go Fish!)

Thursday came and she was all excited about going for that car ride. Would she be as excited when she found out where she was going? I don't think she knew right away, but I put the leash on her and she went happily into the vet hospital.

The news was not good, nothing that couldn't be fixed, but my heart was breaking all the way home. I wasn't sure how my husband would take the news. He didn't like spending money on animals, unlike me, which money was not an object when it came to animals. This is where we differed. It wasn't that I had money, but no amount was too much to spend. So when I told him that Burbank had twenty-three broken teeth and that she would need two root canals on them, he didn't flinch. Just like me he had fallen in love with this dog in a matter of days.

When Dr. Scott told me about her broken teeth, my heart just fell to the floor. The way the teeth were worn, he said she probably chewed her way through a chain collar or a fence. He determined that she was probably six years of age. If he had to guess he would say she was a Rough-coated Retriever. The way she was in the water, I would have to say he was right on the money. My thoughts as I drove back home were mixed. How could anyone treat a dog that badly? This dog didn't have a mean bone in her body. I was angry at the previous owner, but happy that she was about to have the best years of her life. I couldn't imagine the pain she must have been in with the way her mouth was. Before we left the hospital, I had them do all her vaccines and we went home with flea medication. The other issues with her mouth I would have to go home and discuss.

Dr. Scott gave me an estimate for about $2500. When I told Rick how much it could cost us, he said he would pay for half and I would pay the other half. I called for an appointment. Surgery was scheduled for Tuesday. I couldn't wait to get her teeth fixed. She let me look in her mouth and I then saw how worn down all of her front teeth were. I just couldn't imagine the pain she had suffered. My only justification was God sent her to me and she was now going to be taken care of. I truly believe things happen for a reason.

She had gotten a good bill of health other than her teeth, so it was time to introduce her to the house. As always my thoughts were, "Please don't pee in the house," and without hesitation she jumped up the stairs into the house and all she did was sniff around at first, and then she plopped down at our feet. She would get up and follow me around until she figured out I don't sit for very long. She would find Rick and lie down at his feet. She never once tried to jump on any of the couches, but just very content to lie beside a chair. Like I said, as if she had always been ours.

The surgery went off without a hitch. She was bouncing all around and acting normal afterward. The funny thing was you would have thought there was nothing wrong at all with her. She acted the same as she did before the root canals. We had peace of mind knowing her teeth were fixed. We couldn't do anything about her worn down teeth, but that didn't seem to bother her in the least bit.

The first night, she slept in the bedroom next to the bed. I just couldn't believe how well behaved she was. The true test would be other dogs. At the time, I was watching Daisy and Sami a lot, so I was anxious to see how that was going to go.

Daisy was first to meet her. Daisy being the princess that she was, did not like someone else being in her house. Not that it was her house, but don't tell Daisy that. Daisy was always happy to come to my house. She was spoiled. I carried her around like a baby. She had her own toys and she loved to run down the hall to fetch them. Burbank never played with the toys, so I didn't think anything of it.

Daisy didn't like Burbank. She was too much in her face and Burbank was a lot bigger than her. Daisy would growl at first but eventually she knew she would get her way. She would stand up on my leg, my cue to pick her up and carry her around like a baby. Then she would jump on the couch and sit next to me. The first time Burbank saw her up there, she actually barked. First time I heard that. Then when Burbank was sleeping, Daisy would get up and bring me a toy. I would throw that ducky down the hallway and low and behold, Burbank woke up and chased after it. Daisy stopped dead in her tracks as if to say, "Hey, that's mine." She immediately jumped back on the couch and wouldn't play. Spoiled brat. That was my first encounter with how Burbank's thought process was. Let's just say Burbank was not the sharpest tool in the shed. Didn't matter, I loved her even more for that.

As days and visits wore on, Daisy finally figured out that Burbank was always going to be there when she arrived. She eventually got used to her. The only downfall of having Daisy at the house was our sleeping arrangement. Daisy slept in bed with us. The first time Burbank saw that, her paws instantly jumped on the bed as if to say, "Why does she get to sleep up there but I don't?" Burbank would jump up and I'd tell her no and make her get down. This happened for a few minutes, then she finally got the point.

Both dogs would follow us around as we did yard work. Burbank would never wander far from the house, so the idea that she would run away quickly left my thoughts. Even though Burbank loved water, she did not like the swimming pool. She would sit up on the deck, and her fur would get so hot to the touch because she was all black. She never left until I got out of the pool. Daisy soon found out she could go one place that Burbank wouldn't—the pool. Daisy would float around on a raft with me and Burbank would just watch us. Daisy wouldn't go in the creek and we couldn't get Burbank out of it. They found a happy medium to live in peace in the same house together. Once again, all was right in the house.

(Burbank in the backyard, coming back from a walk in the creek)

The next test would be Sami. Sami was a very jealous dog, so I wasn't sure how she was going to react to how close Burbank stuck to my side. The day had come when the two finally got to meet. Burbank was waiting in our kitchen when I pulled into the garage with Sami. Instantly, Sami started to bark. I initially thought the two dogs would get along great. Sami came into the house and started her talking right away. She didn't like Burbank at all, which I found disheartening because I had Sami so much I was hoping the two would get along right away. They were growling and barking at each other. I thought for sure I wasn't going to be able to watch Sami at my house, which would be a shame. We had ten acres for her to run around on, and she loved being there.

I had to break them apart several times. Believe it or not, Sami was the more aggressive one. It took me a good two days to get these two to relax. Once again, the biggest problem we had was instantly Sami jumped on the bed to settle for the night, and Burbank thought, if she's sleeping there, so am I. I tried to reason with Burbank, but to no avail, so from that time on Burbank was in the bed. She would sleep on the floor if we weren't there, but as soon as we were in bed, she was up there with us.

Rick didn't like it very much at first. Okay, let's say not at all, but eventually he came around and Burbank was allowed on the bed. When the two dogs were outside they were terrific together, running and following us all around. Inside it was a little more cramped, and playtime, which was every minute for Sami, became a little more crowded for her liking. Burbank didn't play as long as Sami, she would lie down after the first few throws of the tennis ball or whatever, unlike Sami who never got tired of playing. Sami would get her full day of playing time with or without Burbank.

Mornings were such a ritual at our house. Rick would leave for work at 6 A.M. Burbank would barely lift her head up. She'd get up with me at 7 A.M., go out the front door, pee, and race back into bed. I am not sure about this, but I believe she would lie by the couch all day and wait for us to come home. She didn't like being alone, but she didn't destroy anything when we weren't there, so at my best guess, I would say she slept all day and wait for one of us to come home.

One time, my parents were there and my mom said, "Clair, close the door before the dog gets out." I just started to laugh. Burbank was not going anywhere. We could barely get her to go outside she had become such a homebody.

She loved going for rides. I took her everywhere in the car and she'd even jump up in Rick's truck. Didn't matter which one of us was going, she was going as well. There were times I would take her to Sami's and I would be walking Sami on the leash, and Burbank would just walk right beside us. I never had a leash on her except to go to the vet. I can't believe she and Sami clashed in the beginning because, when either dog met up with any other dogs, they were fine. Like I said, it's just plain jealousy between the two.

She would go to Paul and Lane's with me and get along great with Chip and Bright. Bright Eyes let her know right away who was boss, but Burbank being a little slow, just walked past her and stayed by my side the whole time. She would eventually go outside with Bright and just sit in the yard with her.

It didn't matter where we were, she had gone for a car ride and she was with me. Life was good.

A few years later, Rick and I decided to separate. I was staying with Lane and Paul and Burbank stayed with Rick at the house. I would go back home at noon and let her out and see her, but I felt she should stay with him. They were awfully attached to one another, and at this point Rick needed her more than I did.

I had Bright Eyes to keep me company and Rick had Burbank. If there was a problem, I would come up and take care of her. I missed her but when I would see her, she didn't seem to be sad or upset. She had settled in at the house so well. I don't think she realized anything was wrong. I am sure she did, but it I didn't let myself get upset over not being there. I would see her every day, which was a hike because we lived about 30 miles from Erie, so it would take an hour to drive back and forth every day.

Rick would still go hunting out west every fall, so I would spend a week with her at the house. Eventually, he sold the house and moved back to Erie. He, too, was tired of that drive every day. Now, Burbank lived less than fifteen minutes from me and I saw her whenever I wanted to. As usual, nothing phased her. She would greet me at the door and go outside to pee, and race right back in the house. Rick and I remained close friends, so it was easy to come and go as I pleased. I did his landscaping in his new house and she would sit out front with me the whole time. I would go inside to eat lunch and without hesitation she would sit at my feet. The scenery had changed but everything else remained the same.

Four months after Rick bought his house, Mark and I bought our house. It was, believe it or not, only five minutes from Rick's. So now when Rick would go away for a weekend or go out west hunting, Mark and I would get custody. Once again, Burbank was hanging with Daisy and Sami and a few new ones. All was right in Burbank land once again.

One day, Rick called me and told me that he felt a lump on her side and asked if I could check it out. I felt the lump and called Dr. Scott. It was a mass the size of a half dollar. They removed it and sent it to the lab. We just kept our fingers crossed. The diagnosis was cancer. He thought maybe she had six months to a year to live, depending on how long it took the lump to reappear. Once again upset that this poor dog, who had already been through so much, was in for the fight of her life. Just looking at her you wouldn't know it. Nothing bothered Burbank whatsoever, so when I would look at her I would tell myself that without us, she would have had a terrible life. We gave her a wonderful happy home, so I wasn't going to be upset every time I saw her. We were just going to continue as we had been, that is just life.

Max

My gentlemen's gentleman, a very proud silver Schnauzer: Max. I first met Mary on my walks with Sami. We would be about three houses down and Sami would start to get restless, pulling on the leash the closer we got to this house. She would instantly start barking and suddenly a dog would appear in the door.

This I found out later was Max. Sometimes, he would be outside on his front sidewalk, and other times he would be inside at the front door. You could always see he would run to the back door to be let out so he could come and say hi to us. Max had an invisible fence so he could only go so far. At first, not knowing how Max would react to Sami, I would just let them bark at each other from afar, slowly introducing them day by day. Sami was such a friendly dog she would just want to say hello to every dog then continue on with our walks. As many Sheltie owners know, they are very vocal and you knew when Sami was near your house. They became instant friends.

One day, Mary came out and was talking to me about Sami. I introduced myself and found out Max's name. She thought it was great that I walked dogs, and asked me if she ever needed me could she call me to walk Max. I gave her my number and as the saying goes, the rest was history.

Mary soon called me to walk Max once in a while, and soon I was walking him every day. At some point, Mary decided she was going to go back to work, so then she needed someone to clean for her. It was every other week then John, her husband, decided he wanted me there every week. I got to see Max on a weekly basis along with several walks during the week. Eventually, I started dog sitting when they went out of town, which was happening more frequently since the kids were both in college now. That was perfectly fine with me.

Max was the most well-behaved, easy dog to take care of. You could read him like a book. I knew what he was thinking at all times. I knew when he wanted to eat, go for walks, or just sit and watch TV. He had his own bed, but mostly he would sleep with me, which was a treat for him, because like most dogs, he was not allowed in bed with their owners, but always allowed in bed with the pet sitter.

He was such a proud little thing. He would go on our walks and after he was done doing his business, he would automatically look at it then look up at me as if to say, "Are you going to get that?" I couldn't pick it up fast enough for this little dog. Unlike most dogs, Max would shake uncontrollably in the car. He didn't like going for rides, but once he was where he was going he was fine. It was just that car ride. I never did understand that. I would leave for work in the morning and Max would hop up on the couch and sit on top like he was posing for a magazine, and I swear that was where he would be when I got home. He never got into any trouble, never had any accidents in the house, was kind to everyone and his favorite spot in the house was sitting in front of the glass door looking out. He was so well groomed he looked like he was dressed in a suit every day, never a hair out of place. He liked sitting by you on the couch while you petted his back, perfectly content to be there all night if you were so inclined.

Mary, being the dog lover, saved the diary I left for her the very first time I watched Max. I was grateful because you forget what the dog's reaction is to you the first time you are alone with them and their family is away unless you write it down. Here is what Max was thinking:

Well, you left and I was so sad. I started watching TV, and then the back door opened and it was Mary. I ran over to her and I was happy again. It was a quiet day, but by night I was watching a movie sitting on the couch. Mary cooked dinner and it was fish. I was sitting there staring at her, you know like I normally do, and Mary said I wouldn't like fish. She put some in my food dish and I showed her, I ate it all plus my own food. I was hungrier than I thought. Time to settle down for the night. Hey, what are you doing with my bed? Okay, I will try it. Goodnight.

Sunday morning. Hey, Mary, wake up. It's a new day, let's go. What, get in bed with you. Well, I don't usually, okay, sure. Today it was raining, of course. We went for a walk anyways, my coat got wet. Then we watched golf. Mary fixed lunch and then I got to go for a ride in the car. I sat in Mary's lap the whole way. We went to a graduation party and I was the hit of the party. Well, I think I was, everyone was petting me. I ran around and I was very good, just ask her. Then back in the car and home again. A quick walk before bed. I didn't feel like getting up so Mary carried me to my bed, and fast asleep I went.

Wake up, wake up! We went for our morning walk and, hey, where are we going now?

Oh, you're going to work. I have to stay here, bummer. Okay, see you later. I will watch over the house while you are gone. Mark came home at 11:30 to be with me. Hi, buddy. Then at 12:30 Mary walked in and, hey, she has Sami. Bark! Bark! Bark! We all went for a walk then we stayed at Sami's house. Mary cleaned, and Mark, Sami and I played all afternoon. Sami has a lot of toys like me. We played with them together, playing tug of war together. We got warm so Mary gave us some ice cubes to chew on. Mark went golfing so we ate late. Mark grilled steak and, yes, I looked pathetic and it worked like a charm. Steak in my food dish, yummy! We went for a long walk and then we relaxed in front of the TV, and then I was carried off to bed again. I was carried off to bed again for it was a long day. I was dreaming. I don't remember what it was about, but Mary had to wake me up. I fell asleep again and before I knew it, it was morning.

Tuesday morning. Hmmm, what will we do today? A car ride again and, hey, where are we? It's a bowling alley. I can run around, shut up. This is fun, but I am sticking with you, Mark. I spent the whole morning with Mark and then we went home. Mary must have had to work, so I spent the day with Mark. It's afternoon and Mary is done for the day. We walked over to get Sami and we both got in the car, we both got in the back seat. I looked out one window and Sami looked out the other. We just ran errands, well, Mary ran the errands. Mark stayed in the car with us. It was pretty warm so Mark left the air conditioning on. I would cry every time Mary left the car, and then she would show up and everything would be okay. Sami stayed over and she ate my food. Well, look at her. Does she look like she misses many meals? It was alright, I knew Mary was cooking dinner, hamburgers, so I wasn't afraid of going hungry. We ate, went for our long walk and took Sami home, then settled in for the night. I am so tired after our long days, so I just curl up on the couch till Mary carries me upstairs to bed. I go to sleep wondering what tomorrow will bring.

Good morning, guys. That's right! Let me up on that bed. So what are we doing today? We went for our walk then Mary was off to work. Mark stayed home with me today. We played and Mark read some of his book while I watched out the front door. Mary came home for lunch. Hey, where are you guys going? You forgot me. I'll sleep a little to catch up on my daily nap. Mark and Mary went golfing. It was hot. They probably wish they were here with me where it's nice and cool. Yeah, yeah, you are home. What's for dinner? Chicken, that's funny, it's my favorite. I know I told you it was hamburgers. That was yesterday, today it's chicken. No, I don't want my teeth cleaned. If you can catch me, you can clean them. Oh, darn, you're fast. Okay, okay, but I am not going to like it. We ate then we went for nightly walk. Mary picked me up and I fell asleep in her lap. Then she fell asleep in Mark's lap. We decided to go to bed since we were all sleeping anyway.

Let me up on the bed. Mark has to work but Mary is staying home with me. We stayed in bed for a little bit longer. I curled up right next to Mary and off to snooze land I went. We were both pretty lazy. It was a nice morning. We played and sat outside. Another hot one. Then she had to go to work. She left at 11:30 and Mark came home at 12:30. I don't even have time to nap with these two. We are just waiting for Mary. I just rest with Mark on the couch. Mary's home. She brought pizza home for dinner. I ate my food, Mary said pizza would upset my stomach so I didn't get any. We got in the car after dinner and looked at all the people. Where are we? Come on, let me out, let me out, I want to go. We were at the peninsula and we were off on our walk. People on bikes, roller blades and walking. My God, I'm exhausted. My head's on the pillow and I am sleeping. Another good day.

It's early Friday, and I mean early, 3 A.M., and I woke Mary up. It's thundering. Okay, if you insist, I'll get in bed with you. I'm up, I'm down, yes, rub that spot on my belly. Ah, that's good. I am sleeping, what storm, no problem. Sun's out now and we are walking. I went to work with Mark and Mary went in her car. We had a quiet day, but then I went to Mark's softball game and once again I was the center of attention. Everybody thought I was such a cool dog. They really liked me a lot. Well, who could blame them? Look at me. Once again, I was tired. The game lasted about three hours. I fell asleep in the car on Mary's lap. What a fun day that was. Hmmm, what will tomo—snore, snore, snore.

Another sunny day today. Come on, let's go for our walk. Well, guys, what are we going to do today? Oh, I forgot to tell you something. When Sami and I were walking by our house she started to go nuts, barking and running. I just looked at her and said, I am right here, dummy. She was calling for me to come out and I was standing right next to her. Anyways, today is Saturday and we are back in the car. I don't think I've ever gone for so many car rides in one week. We went to a birthday party and the people had a fenced-in yard so I got to run around and chase all the little kids. We were there all day. After the softball game last night and the birthday party today, I was exhausted. I was on the couch taking a nap and Mary said they were going to a Seawolves game and I would have to stay home. I didn't care, I just lay back down and slept. They came home early. They got cold, lucky for me. We went for a walk and then it was bedtime.

Sunday. It's our usual day. Coffee and TV, and because it's raining, we took our walk later.

I'm acting funny today, suitcases were being taken out and put into the car. Mary's cleaning our house and I am not quite sure what's going on, but something's up. Hey, what's that noise? It's the garage door. You're home, you're home. Come on, sit down, I will tell you all about it. I'm glad you're home.

Love,

Max

(Max posing on the couch, looking sweeter than ever)

Just about every six months I would get to watch Max. The next time I watched him, however, I had already made plans to be away for the weekend. We had tickets to see the Lion King in Buffalo, so we went up the night before to stay at the casino. We left Saturday and came home on Sunday night. I told Mary that I already had these plans, but maybe I could find someone to watch Max for the weekend. I could be with him all week and be back on Sunday. Mary agreed and I told her that Mark had an employee that often watched our cats. I talked to Brianna and she said she could watch Max for me.

She came over and Max liked her, not that I thought it would go any other way, but I was funny about who was watching the dogs. He's not even my dog, but I felt responsible because he was in my care. Max was with me all week, then we left at 1 P.M. I called Brianna at 5 to check on them. They were watching TV and Max was on the couch with her. All was well. I worried all night. It was May 4 and over the night we had a snowstorm that dumped about eight inches on us.

Getting around Buffalo was no fun. We were used to the snow, but it was a freak snowstorm so we weren't dressed for it at all. My biggest worry wasn't if we would get home okay, but when would I get home to Max. They shut down Interstate 90 because of so many accidents. We went down to Rte 20 and we were on our way. I called Brianna after the play and she said everything was great. Max was doing fine. I told her I wasn't sure when we would get home because of the weather and she said it wasn't even bad in Erie. They might have gotten four inches at best, so we knew once we got out of Buffalo we would run out of the storm. Four hours later, we were driving into Erie. Normally, it would take an hour and a half, but because of the snow storm it took forever.

If you don't already know this, Erie has the prettiest sunsets. I can't remember where, but it was an article in a magazine that read, Hawaii was number one, China was number two, and Erie was voted number three for the most beautiful sunsets. This never fails to amaze me.. So when we drove into town, after that awful snow storm, the sunset was beautiful. After four hours of scary nail-biting weather and roads, we were back in town and Max was fine. As I knew he would be. You can talk to me till you're blue in the face, and I will still not relax until I am back with the animals where I am suppose to be.

I made sure this didn't happen again. I told my clients they had to tell me as soon as they knew when they are going out of town. This way the animals are always in my care and I can still plan my life around them.

Once again, I find myself with Max, and this is what happened this time.

Well, it's 7:30 and I am sitting here watching cartoons. I like Spongebob, but not Dora.

Bark, bark! Hi, hi, hi. Yes, Mom and Dad left again. But it's okay because I knew you would show up. Yep, I am ready for my morning walk, let's go! Mary had some Lucky Charms for breakfast; me I like the marshmallows. Where are you going? Oh, okay, but change the channel. Someone's here. It's Mark. You just missed Mary. Another walk, sure I would love one. Mark is with me the rest of the day, so I think I will take a nap.

Mary's home and, hey, who's there? Sami! Hi, Sami. Yeah, come in. Why are you here? Oh, I see, you are here to eat my food. What's the matter, don't you get fed where you live? Hey, you ate it all. Good thing Mary's cooking something because I may have starved. I will climb up here and see if I can smell what's for dinner tonight. Mary, paw, paw, I am right here. What's for dinner? Mmmm, rigatoni. Let me just see, that's right, put it right in my bowl.

Yes, yes, I love it. Have any meatballs to go with that? A walk for all of us, absolutely. Sami and I have full bellies, so yes, let's go.

Now where are you going? I don't think I like bowling season. Oh, Mark is staying home with me. Okay, bye. Is it 9 P.M. already? Didn't even miss you. A bath? No, thanks. Oh, you meant you, okay. Carry me to bed, Mary. Goodnight, guys.

It's morning. I know it's 6:45. I am going to Mark's side of the bed, nothing. Mary, come on, get up. Oh, that's even better, put me here, right in the middle. I am snuggling in between them. Time to get up. Oh, that's good, lick, lick, lick. Peanut butter, it's one of my favorites. Every morning, I get a finger size lick of PB. It's a great morning snack. Yes, bark, bark! Let's go for our morning walk. Hi, Bailey, yellow Lab down the street. No, we have to keep moving, but have a good day, anyways. They have to go to work today, okay, but don't put Dora on. Yeah, yeah, Katie Couric—hot one. Mark's home, you don't work that much, do you? It was a little on the stormy side today, but I am on a walk so I don't care. Mark said I did fine on my walk.

What's for dinner? Yes, I know I have food in my bowl, just let me sniff your food to see if I might like yours better. Maybe Sami will come over and eat my food every day, so I can get human food. That's right, put in my bowl, mmm. Stuffed peppers with no peppers, just the hamburger and rice. I think that's healthy for me. Wait, where are you going now? I definitely don't like bowling season. You both bowl on Thursdays. Alright, but come right home, not going out for drinks after. Hi, where's Mark? Oh, you bowl at different times. I will go for a quick walk. Oooh, it's dark, alright, I am coming. It's pretty late. Is Mark coming home? You're home, okay, carry me to bed.

I am right here in the middle of the bed. It was stormy so I just jumped up on the bed. A walk, are you crazy, it's raining. I don't walk in the rain. I can hold it, really. Alright, but I am not going to like it. Shake, walk, shake walk, poop, walk. Shake, come on, Mary, run. I am soaked, shake. One final shake and then, yeah, get that towel out. My coat is all wet, yeah, that was fun—-not.

Do you have to work every day? Hi, Mark. Mary and Sami walked in shortly after Mark. Let's go to your house so I can eat all your food. Figure nothing's in her bowl. Come on, I'll chase you around your house. I know I will shake, too. I got wet on the walk over here, second time today. I like coming here, you have some nice toys. Back to my place, sure Sami, you can come over, too. Now you want my chewy bone, typical girl—mine, mine, mine. One more walk, Sami has to go home, but she can come back. Where are you going? Can I sit up front with you? Okay, that's better. Hey, I recognize this place. Bark, bark, bark! Whine, whine. Jump over to Mark's lap. It's the bowling alley. Let's go, what do you mean no? Too many people. I won't bite anyone. Cry, cry, cry. Alright, stay where I can see you. Yeah, quit waving at me and come and get me already. I am fine, but why couldn't I—oh, alright, I'll let it go. Come on, you promised me some, mmm, vanilla. Love, lick, lick, lick! Vanilla ice cream! It's been a long day. Think I will jump up on the couch and go to—carry me.

Saturday morning and Mark is up and it's early. Okay, I will keep her warm. Put me right up there, yeah, yeah, bye. Back to sleep for Mary and me. Stretch, it's sunny, yeah, let me just grab your sneaker for you. Catch me, no really catch me—alright, you can have it if you can catch me! I am walking now and it's sunny and Mary's home with me all day. I got to sleep in bed with Mary today, not much different than having Mark. I too have a mustache and let's face it, I am better-looking than Mark. It's a good day, a ride, cry, whine, bark. I can go into Country Fair, why can't I? Take that back, I am not Psycho. I just want to go. Milk, that's all, is that for our cereal? Okay, I'll behave.

I am not acting weird. How would you know, you were working all day? Alright, let's go outside. What's a Midol? Do I take those, Mom? I'm lying in the sun, playing dead dog in the front yard. It's just that kind of day. Are you eating? No more dead dog, alive and wanting a cracker. Nope, there's nothing I won't eat, haven't you figured that out by now? It's my metabolism, that's how I keep my boyish figure. What a relaxing day. I am up here, lying in Kevin's bedroom in the sun, it feels so good. Let me be, I'm good.

It is 6:45, let me up there in that bed. Ah, just what the doctor ordered. Heavy sigh, head down and my eyes are heavy. No, don't zip up that suitcase. Look, I am

looking really cute, don't pack. Okay, but I am coming with you. Leave room in the back seat. Watching TV and I fell asleep. Hey, Mom and Dad are home. Everything is good in the world.
Love,
Max

I moved into my new house in Erie and Max now comes to stay at my house. It's a nice change of pace for him. Not only does Mary and John get away, but Max goes on vacation from his house as well.

Most of my dogs are now coming to the house. Just a few want me to stay in their homes. It's really nice for me and the dogs. They get a change of scenery and I get to be home and take care of things at home. He likes coming to my house and going places. He just doesn't like that car ride. He likes going, just not getting there. He is so easy to take with me anywhere because he's great with adults and children. He is such gentlemen's gentleman, he doesn't bark, pull on his leash, he is just a great dog. They don't get any better than Max, the ultimate human dog. You know what I mean. If he were human, I would compare him to Richard Gere in "Pretty Woman": distinguished, smart, on top of his game.

(Max at my house on the big chair)

One day, I was walking Max and he started to cough. He then spit up some saliva. I didn't think anything of it. I figured he ate some grass or just drank a little too much water as dogs tend to do. I didn't mention it to Mary, thinking nothing of it. As weeks passed, he started to cough more frequently, often bringing up phlegm. The spit up was now yellow in color. Concerned, I talked to Mary that day and she said she noticed he was coughing, and to me he seemed to be losing a little weight as well. He of course was always that slim and trim great-looking dog, so when he lost weight it showed through his sides. I don't remember the day exactly, but I do remember the phone call between Mary and myself.

Max was in the beginning stages of congenital heart failure. Of course, Mary was so upset when she was talking to me, she could barely get the doctor's report out. I believe that was in October. The doctors told Mary that six months at best. Mary and John were heartbroken. As most dogs are family members, Max was special. The kids had their senior portraits on the walls, and in this house, Max's professional portrait was next to the kids'. There are dogs and then there are special dogs. Max was right up there on the family tree. Every family portrait that was taken, Max was front and center. I didn't see Max as the family pet; I saw Max as the youngest member of the family. Hence, this news was devastating at best. The doctor's recommendation was to keep Max on a strict bland diet, medication, and very little exercise. Walks would be too hard on his heart.

I would clean the house every Tuesday. Max would still follow me around, then he would just get tired and lie down in each room. Many times he would be down on the rug in front of the door and just watch out the front door. Mary and John took one more vacation after his diagnosis. She was very nervous to leave him, but she knew he was in good hands. He was on a chicken and rice, or hamburger and rice diet. No walks, just going out in the backyard, and very few car rides. I was nervous that because he gets upset in the car, maybe it would be too hard on his heart. I am no doctor, but when he shakes so much I would think it would be hard on his heart. So I only took him for rides if I wasn't going anywhere for long. Mary would call everyday she was away to check on him. The answer was always the same, he's quiet but good.

Max's cough was getting more frequent. Even with the medication he seemed to be struggling. It was hard to see him like this. I would go over and pet his back while he coughed just so he knew I was there.

It was like when I was a kid and had the flu. My mother would hold my hair back. I knew she was there for me and it was comforting. So I was there for Max and hope that he felt comforted as well.

The months were passing by. Mary was taking great care of Max, never missing a beat. Medications and doctor's appointments were kept and met. I can't be sure of this, but I am positive there were many nights that Mary would sleep on the couch just to be close to Max, the ultimate human devotion.

It was now May and Max was about the same. Although very thin, glad that it was summer. Emily and Kevin were home from college so someone was home with Max every day now. Max was slowing down more and more each day. He was diagnosed in October and now it was June. The doctors said six months and it was now eight months. I can only credit Mary and John with such great care of Max. One Tuesday, I was cleaning and Max was following me around. The kids were out back sitting on chaise chairs in the sun. They stay out of my way when I am there. Max was lying in his special place in the hallway in front of the door. I was lying right in front of him petting him and I remember Emily walked by and said to me, "You are too much." She was laughing because I was supposed to be cleaning and instead I was lying on the floor with Max.

I watched Max every Tuesday, but this particular Tuesday as I was lying on the floor with him and this was our conversation: "Max, I know you are tired. I can see in your eyes you just don't feel good. You've lived two months longer than you were supposed to. You have put up a strong fight, but it's okay to let go now. I will miss you, but I want you to be healthy and happy by Rainbow Bridge. It's okay to let go." I kissed his head, told him I loved him, and finished cleaning. No one heard that conversation; it was just between me and Max. I didn't know what would happen, I just wanted Max to know it was okay.

Mary called me Tuesday night. When I heard her voice on the phone, it was dead silence. Then she found her voice, "Mary, the family has talked and we think it is time to take Max in and end his suffering."

I started to cry for Max and Mary because I knew how hard this call was to make. She said, "I am calling because I wanted you to have a chance to come over tonight and say goodbye." I then told her about our conversation on the rug that day and that I already said my goodbyes. She was astonished. She said, "How did you know?" I just shook my head and said, "I just knew."

Max's portrait hangs on the wall still today. His ashes in a specially made urn, with a picture of him painted on the front, are in a glass armoire in the family room. Sitting next to the urn is a wonderful picture of Max when he was younger. We still talk about Max today and I dust his picture every week, and look at him with fond memories. Max may be gone, but his memory will last a lifetime.

(Max as his dapper self)

Then there was Gunnar...

Chelsea

(Two Best Buds!)

It was April again and this meant I was going to get Chelsea for ten days. This time she was coming to my house for the first time. She was very excited when I came and got her for a car ride. She loved going for a ride. She came right in the house and made herself at home. She liked that she didn't have to go up any stairs to go to bed. She tried to get up on the couch, and seeing as it was new, I made her get down. She didn't mind being on the floor. It was carpeted and she just lay there and watched us. If we got up she was up. She stood at the top of the stairs to the basement when I would go and get the laundry, she wanted to come down, but just didn't want to go up and down the stairs if she didn't have to.

We didn't have a bed for her to sleep in, so Mark and I took her to Pet Smart and bought her a bed. That didn't take long for her to snuggle in for the night. We bought her the bed because she would put her front paws on our bed as if she was going to jump up and go to sleep. Mark said no because she was just too big to sleep in the bed. If you are more than 10 pounds you don't sleep in bed with us. So her new bed was just fine. We bought her some new toys, which she loved. She had a new football and would carry it around with her wherever she went in the house. That quickly became her favorite.

(Chelsea and her new toy)

She was so smart. Ellise really trained her well. She could sit, lie down, and play dead. She quickly got attached to us and our way of life. She knew that on Mondays and Thursdays, she was going to Lane and Paul's to hang out with Bright Eyes. These were her favorite days. She would lay out in the yard for hours just watching people and traffic go by. If other dogs walked by, she would get up and walk over to them to check them out. She quickly got to know everyone in our neighborhood.

Our walks were pretty slow and she would feel the need to say hello to everyone who was outside, so a walk around the block lasted as if we walked four miles. It would literally take us forty-five minutes to go around the block. She was great with other dogs, people, kids, you name it. She was your typical Lab, a cuddly teddy bear. Some nights we would be up late, she would get up and look at us, we would say, "Chelsea, go to bed. It's okay." She would walk very slowly down the hallway, but because we didn't join her, she would walk back out and lie on the floor again. Some nights we'd be playing until 3 A.M. She would just put herself to bed. She would be so tired from the day's activities and just couldn't hang with us for that long.

She got to be so comfortable with us and our house that she didn't want to go back home. Ellise came to pick her up and she would be excited to see her, but she would be depressed when she went home. Because Ellise worked all day, she would be alone for long periods of time. At our house, she would go to work with me a lot and if she wasn't with me, she would be with Mark at the bowling alley. She loved going there because she would go right to the kitchen for her piece of cheese or ham. She would walk around and say hello to all the senior bowlers and then lie behind the desk with Mark. She was with someone all the time.

I got a call about three days after she went home. Ellise said to me, "Mary, I work a lot of hours and Chelsea seems to be so happy with you guys. Would you consider keeping her?" I couldn't believe it. I never thought Ellise would give her up. I was so excited. I was happy for me, but even happier for Chelsea. I told her I would have to talk to Mark first and I would call her back. That night we went and picked up Chelsea to bring her to her new home. This was so hard on Ellise, but she knew she would be better off in a house that doesn't have stairs. Chelsea was getting older and her arthritis was getting worse. As hard as it was for her to give her up, she wasn't thinking of herself right now; she was thinking of Chelsea.

That's what makes a great dog owner. She knew she could come see her anytime, and whenever I would go to Ellise's, she would come with me and pick up right where she left off. Ellise would come see her and Chelsea was happy to see her every time. But she didn't want to leave with her. She was home and she loved it.

We went out and bought her an orthopedic bed hoping it would help with her stiffness. She stepped right up on it and curled up for the night. It had such a great cushion on it, and I do believe it did help with her joints. She eventually had a basket full of toys that she would share with whoever came over. I would take her with me to Sami's on Mondays and Fridays, and to Lane and Paul's on Mondays and Thursdays. When I didn't take her, she would lick that sore on her leg. I do believe it was just out of boredom that she started licking it, but it became so sore I think she would lick it to try and make it feel better. It just became a habit after so long. So we would leave and I would wrap it. Most times, she got the wrap off, which upset us, so we would leave it on and only take it off when she went to bed to give it air.

It was July and we always go to Florida. This year, however, we now have a dog. Diana was living with us at the time so we asked her if she would watch her and she said yes. Chelsea was easy so she didn't mind. We were sitting at Tampa Bay Rays game and you know it's pretty loud in the dome, so when Diana called all I heard was, "Chelsea got hit by a truck." My heart stopped and I said to Mark, "Get out in the hall so we can hear what she is saying." I was so upset running out into the hall. Then when we got out there, Diana said, "No, Dad, not hit by a truck. She was sprayed by a skunk." I just started laughing just out of shear thankfulness that she didn't get hit by a truck. So I told her what to do and she did, but she said it didn't work and she was going to leave Chelsea in the garage overnight. I felt so bad for both Diana and Chelsea. Chelsea didn't know why she wasn't allowed in the house and Diana was freaking over the smell.

She called the vet and they told her what to do to get that smell out. I swear every time Chelsea got wet, she still smelled like skunk for at least two months after that. Diana was so upset she said that was the worst time of her life. I just said if that was the worst she would ever go through, she should consider herself lucky. Needless to say, she did not appreciate that at all. She was glad to see us home and her dog sitting days were over.

(Burbank, Grandpa and Chelsea)

It was fall and time for Rick to go out west hunting again. That meant that I got Burbank for ten days. It was great having Chelsea and Burbank together. Chelsea had short, black hair and Burbank had long, black hair. They both had the Lab face and they were about the same weight. They got along great. It was like having a mirror of each other around. Burbank also went with me to all the houses. Sami, of course, would bark but then would get used to the other dogs being around. It was funny because they were all very similar in the fact that they all felt the need to be number one in my book, and fought over who was going to be closer to me at all times. Eventually, Sami would win because the other two would poop out and finally lay down.

Sami would bark and that would make Burbank bark, though she didn't know why she was barking, she was just talking back to Sami. Chelsea would look up but would go no further with that.

These days were my favorite because all three dogs were by my side. I was in my glory, the more dogs, the happier I was. Chelsea and Burbank didn't need leashes, but Sami would, so I could take all three dogs for a walk at the same time.

It was interesting on Mondays and Thursdays because at one point I had Sami, Burbank and Chelsea all in my car going over to see Bright Eyes. It looked like a doggy day care when we would all go for a walk around the property. All the dogs had been to Lane and Paul's so they knew the walk well. And you would have to add Chip the Beagle to the mix because, undoubtedly, he would be there also. As we all walked together, I would just smile at how fortunate I was to have such a great job. Life just couldn't get any better than that.

Shortly after this, Sami had moved to Gettysburg, so I was down to Bright Eyes, Chelsea, Chip, and sometimes, Burbank. Chelsea and Bright Eyes were really good together. They both would lie outside and just watch time pass by. They loved sitting in the sun. What a life. I'd walk the dogs when I was done cleaning, kiss Bright Eyes and tell her I loved her and put her back in the house. I would put Chelsea in the car and we would be on our way home for the day. This was an every Monday and Thursday ritual that Chelsea loved. Our time spent together with Bright Eyes was very special. We loved these days.

Burbank

(My forever faithful friend, always by my side)

I have been going over and letting Burbank out every day during lunch. I have noticed lately she hasn't been coming out to greet me at the door when I came in and she is very slow in getting up. I knew time was not her friend, but I was not making that decision. Rick had called me and said she was throwing up her food lately and her energy level has really gone down. I told him that the tumor was probably growing and it was going to be hard for her to cope every day now. He asked me when we should make the decision to put her down and I told him he would know when it was time.

Rick called me on March 18 and said she didn't do well over the weekend, so he felt it was time. He didn't think he would be able to take her. He couldn't do it emotionally, not physically. I told him I wouldn't have it any other way.

I began to cry thinking of our journey together. She had such a bad life before I found her, but what a great life ever since. Without the tumor, I believe she could still be with us. But such as it was, I picked her up on Monday morning and she spent the day with me. She liked going to Paul and Lane's, like all my other dogs did. Nancy stopped by and I told her I had an appointment for her that evening. She didn't understand because she was getting around so well and she seemed good to her. I made her feel her side and she felt the tumor that had grown back to about the size of a football.

Just as she has always done, she followed me around the whole day. It made me rethink my plan for the evening, but as the day went on she laid in the kitchen on the floor where it was cool. She would drink some water then throw it right back up, once again reaffirming that our decision was the right one. As you can imagine, my thoughts go back to the day I found her and all the great days she has had since then. I wished I would have had her from a puppy, but sometimes dogs choose us and not the other way around. It's usually a blessing that they do, and certainly she chose the right people to care for her in her last five years.

I had called Rick before I took her and asked if he wanted me to drive by the house before I took her, and he said no. He had said goodbye in the morning and that's how he wanted to remember her. Then he choked up and asked that I get her ashes returned so he could keep them. I had already made up my mind before he had asked for them, but I was glad that he requested them. At that moment, I realized just how much she meant to him. He never was an emotional person, but this particular dog really got to his heart. It did my heart good just to hear that.

As hard as it was for me to take the animals in for their final drive, I wouldn't have it any other way. As we sat in the waiting room to be called back, I petted her and talked about the old days. Knowing she was a little anxious to be in the hospital, just my soothing voice and hand on her calmed her down. It was now our turn to go back and I walked her back. The staff was always very quiet when they were talking to you. They knew all too well how hard this could be and tried to make it as easy on the client as they did on the pet. We got all the questions out of the way and then we just waited for the doctor to come in. She had lost so much weight so I told them I would like her to be on the table so she could lie in my arms as she went out.

My conversation with Burbank was the same as it is with all the dogs I take in. As she was lying in my arms, I whispered in her ear. "Sweetie, this is the last time you will ever have to lay on this table, I promise. When you get to where you are going, I want you to find PT. He will look after you. I have already asked him to do this for me, so he is waiting for you. Your Dad and I have loved you since the day you hopped in my car at the bank, and we thank you so very much for coming into our lives." As the tears ran down my face, my voice was still calm and I was not sure how the doctors got through days like this, but they did, and Dr. Scott has been through this with me quite a few times, so he was used to my emotional breakdowns.

I don't think he would have it any other way. My conversation with Burbank continued, "You were one of the best dogs I have ever had and I thank you for your loyalty and your love." As her panting slowed down and her eyes closed, I told her the tumor would be gone soon and she would soon be able to run again and feel as she had when she was running in the creek on one of our many walks. "Remember, go find PT and run with him. I love you. I will see you again. Wait for me."

Two weeks have passed and I picked up Burbank's ashes and took them over to Rick. He has decided to take them out west with him when he moves. I smiled and said, "She would love that."

Stripes and BB

(Our newest babies)

Nancy and Steve always got stray kitties in their barn, but there was one that was probably the ugliest cat I have ever seen. She was so ugly she was cute. She had every color all over her face, black, brown, white and orange. She was so nice we all fed her because we all felt sorry for her. She was in the barn but all she wanted was to be loved. She would come right up to Heidi when she was outside, and Heidi would just let her. When Nancy would take Heidi for her morning walks, this cat would go on the walks with them and follow them all around. Nancy would feed her every day, and one day she realized she was having kittens of her own. At this time, she probably wasn't even one year herself, but she was definitely having a litter. We joked because we couldn't imagine what they were going to look like. Nancy had seen a white cat hanging around the barn, so she suspected they would have some white on them along with all of mom's freaky colors.

It was June and Kiki (that's what they decided mom's name should be) was really heavy with kittens. Nancy was worried about her, so they moved her from the barn into a room next to the garage with a box and blanket. I was a little worried because she was so big I just hoped she wasn't going to have any problems with the birth. She would waddle around and then finally she had the little ones. She had three multi-colored ones, two orange and white ones, and an all-black one. At first, she was taking care of them, but then she stopped, so Nancy brought them into her house and blocked them off so she had the whole foyer. It was clean and she could come and go as she needed to without the kittens getting out.

When I am there every other week cleaning, I am getting attached to all of them. Heidi was also attached she would constantly walk up to the gate and check things out. As they got older, the kittens would sometimes climb out and lie next to Heidi. She was so motherly with them. One day, I just went home and asked Mark if we could have two of the kittens. Of course, he said yes. He never says no to me, but I always ask just in case. So now the question was which color I was going to choose. I changed my mind every time I was in the house. They were eight weeks old and they were ready to come home, so we had to make the decision. We told Jesse one of the cats would be his, so he came out and picked out the orange and white one, which was a boy. I decided that we would take a multi-colored one because I wanted to have a girl. Jesse named his cat Stripes, and I told Mark I would like to name our kitty, BB, after Burbank. He just smiled and agreed.

We came in with the two kittens and Chelsea instantly came to greet them, sniff, sniff, and it was love at first sight.. They laid by Chelsea every time they could. BB was often nose to nose and that was how they slept. Chelsea loved the kitties. She would sometimes chase them but it was all in fun. Stripes would get in Chelsea's bed with her and sleep curled up next to her belly. Bella, on the other hand, was not so happy at first.

Let me explain who Bella is. My girlfriend Julie called me; she's another animal lover who always calls me when she finds an animal. She tells me her mother-in-law heard a cat in the tree and she got it down. It was a tiny little kitty and they fed her and put her in the barn with their cows. She didn't mind the cows at all. Julie called me and asked me if I would like her, and of course, hearing the story I couldn't turn her down. So I went out and bought everything I would need and then drove out to the country to get her. At the time, I had Sami and Chelsea so we would see how she would do. We took her out of the cage and the dogs were of course very interested in the little furry thing that crawled out of the carrier. She was so stinking cute and she didn't even pay attention to the dogs, much to their discontent.

Mark came home and just did one of his "ah" sighs, so I knew she was in like Flynn. Our daughter came home and she had just broken up with her long-time boyfriend, and Mark and I just looked at each other and handed the kitty to her. She named her Bella. She was our cat for a day. Now she was Diana's. She lived with us for six months before we brought in Stripes and BB. She was not happy at first, then it was love once she got to know the little ones.

(Stripes, BB, and Bella getting closer by the day.)

We had to acclimatize the cats at an early age because we knew they would have to get along with many dogs if they wanted to survive living in our house. Unfortunately, they have no idea what they are in for. We have so many dogs that come and go, we hope that with Chelsea's help they will learn to love dogs as much as we do

There are not too many dogs that the cats don't get along with. BB is more afraid of the smaller dogs and Stripes is afraid of the bigger dogs, until they are with them for about a day or two, then it's all good again. BB doesn't really have time for any of the dogs except Chelsea, and Stripes likes them all.

I am sure that every time my front door opens the kittens are wondering who is coming through that door now. They are always ready to run to the basement where they hide out until they feel safe. Every day is an adventure for them.

As time goes on and I watch more and more dogs, BB still likes the big dogs and Stripes loves the little dogs. BB will slink around all the Golden Retrievers and hiss at all the little dogs. Stripes will run past the little dogs in hopes that a chase will be in the air, and it almost always is. Stripes will stay downstairs if there are big dogs upstairs. They are brother and sister and yet they are extremely different in every way. They keep us guessing.

(Still close even though we are brother and sister)

Chelsea

(Chelsea with her football and Stripes playing with her tail)

I was so excited in August we were going on a cruise, and it was Mark's first cruise. We went a day early, so on Saturday morning at 4:30 A.M., we were all packed up and Diana took us to the airport. She was watching Chelsea again for us and she said, "I will watch her but she better not get sprayed by a skunk again." So off we went. Saturday by the pool in Orlando, I told Mark, "Oh, my God, I never said goodbye to Chelsea." I felt terrible I was so excited. I completely left without kissing her. I have never done that ever. Mark said it will be fine.

So don't you know we get a call around 6 P.M. and it's Diana. She's crying and can't even talk. Chelsea couldn't get up. She called the vet. On Saturdays and Sundays, we had an animal emergency room, and because it was Saturday, she took her there. She told us she had had a stroke.

I was so upset I couldn't stop crying. I just knew it. I had a funny feeling, and what made me think of her in the afternoon? I was able to talk to the doctor and he informed me that Chelsea had a mild stroke and he was sure she would make a full recovery. She would need special care and time. We couldn't not go on the cruise and here was Mark with me crying at this end, and on the other end his daughter, who vowed never to watch Chelsea again, crying the whole time. Mark managed somehow to calm me down and I asked Diana to bring Chelsea home and just make sure she was comfortable and resting, no long walks and keep her quiet for the whole week. If she felt she needed help, I told her to call Lane. Even though this was Lane and Paul's busy time, I knew she would help if I needed her. It was too late in the evening to call Lane, so I would call her in the morning and tell her what was happening. I was still upset but felt somewhat comforted with what the doctor had told me. I did sleep but it was a long night.

The next day we were on the bus going to the port, and I thought I should call Lane and fill her in on what had happened with Chelsea..When I called her it was odd, because she wasn't at work.. It was Sunday and she was always at work by 10 A.M. I left a message with the girl that answered the phone to have Lane call me when she got in. When I hung up the phone, I told Mark that Lane wasn't in yet, and just thought to myself that that was really weird. About an hour passed and my phone finally rang. It was Lane. She said, "Why are you calling me? You are supposed to be on vacation." That's when I told her what had happened to Chelsea, and asked her if Diana had any questions or any more problems could Diana call her if she needed her help?

Lane was great with dogs and Chelsea was so comfortable around Lane. I actually would feel better if she was in Lane's care. She said, "Yes, Diana could call her if she needed anything". Then I said to her, "By the way, why were you so late getting to work?" Not that that was any of my business, it was just very odd. I am not sure why I asked her that, but somehow felt the need to. Her response was, "Mary, I didn't want to tell you while you were on vacation. We had to put Bright Eyes down this morning." I just looked out the bus window and the tears began to flow again. There was complete silence on the phone for a moment. She said, "Mary, are you okay?" I said yes, as best as I could, then asked her the same question. She said it was time, that Bright Eyes just couldn't get up from a lying position and her quality of life was no longer what it used to be.

We both cried on the phone for a few minutes and then she said, "Don't think about it, have a great vacation and we will see you when you get back." I shook my head but still couldn't speak a word. I didn't feel bad that I didn't get to say goodbye to Bright Eyes because I did that every time I left her. Because I didn't get to say goodbye to PT, I made sure that every time I leave my dogs, I kiss them and tell them I love them because you just never know. This way they always know how I feel and I can't say that I didn't say goodbye. Except I didn't say goodbye to Chelsea the day before, and this upset me even more. She hated when we left her and I should have been more aware of that.

Have we tried to comfort her before we left, maybe she wouldn't have had a stroke. These were the thoughts that were going through my head as we were on the bus leaving for vacation. I felt helpless. I couldn't be there for Lane or Diana. I had to try and get myself together to go on this cruise that we had planned for a year for. I wasn't going to ruin Mark's time by crying. He just rubbed my back understanding how I felt and knowing there was nothing we could do.

Wednesday, we were in Jamaica and we could get a call out to Diana with our cell phone. She said Chelsea was doing good and she was taking her medicine. She had taken her to the vet for her recheck and the doctor still believed she would make a full recovery. The vacation went well, started off terrible, but finished well.

My main concern was set on seeing Chelsea as soon as we got home. We pulled up and Chelsea was sitting in the yard as she always did. As soon as I got out of the car, I ran over to her. She got up slowly and she was very excited to see us. She looked great. That was exactly what I wanted to see. I kissed her and told her we were sorry she went through that without us, but we knew she would pull through and she did. Now that I could see for myself that Chelsea was better and on the mend, my mind immediately went to my original ball of sunshine–Bright Eyes.

Bright Eyes

(Me and Bright looking pretty in the garden)

That night we got home from vacation, I called Lane to see how she and Paul were doing. She said she felt so terrible about telling me while I was on vacation. I told her I would have been mad had she not told me. I need to hear the good news and the bad news. They need to know that I am thinking about them during this sad time in their lives. I was with Bright Eyes for all of her years, through the good and bad, and I would have been mad if she wouldn't have told me. I understand her reasoning behind not telling me, but in my mind, I could look up at the stars and talk to Bright and know that she was listening.

We talked some more and she was very sad to say the least, but she also knew it was time as we often do, and that she was in a much better place and she was healthy and happy and with her brother, PT. I knew the next day that I would be at their house to clean and that's when it would hit me the hardest, so I wasn't looking forward to tomorrow. I knew once again that I would be working with tears and swollen eyes all day.

Monday afternoon and I was sitting in the driveway to Lane and Paul's house. I must have sat there for at least half an hour before walking into the house. I opened the door that Bright Eyes sat in front of for most of her life. This was probably her favorite place to lie. I walked in and lost it. The tears just started to flow. I couldn't believe that I was never going to see Bright Eyes again. I walked around the house just picturing Bright in all her favorite spots. Her bed was still in the living room where it had been her whole life. She wasn't there. Paul and Lane's ray of sunshine had moved on to another life.

I can't say I didn't say goodbye because I had every Monday and Thursday for the last twelve years of her life. Ever since we lost PT, I kiss all the dogs goodbye and tell them I love them. So I knew Bright Eyes knew how I felt and I believe in my heart that she's healthy, happy, and running around in a field with her brother, somewhere waiting for me to come and walk them again.

A few days later, a tree was delivered to be planted on the grounds in Bright Eyes's memory. It was from the staff of the Vet Hospital. When I worked there, they had never in my memory ever sent a gift like this to anyone. What a great heartfelt gesture this was, and I was very impressed. The tree is planted in the front of the house where the driveway circles around. You can see it and think of Bright when you come and when you leave. The driveway is a never-ending circle, eternity.

A couple weeks before Bright Eyes left us, Lane had some portraits done of her. Every picture was a great shot of her. I just smiled. There were pictures of her in the lawn, sitting by the back door, and pictures with Lane.

Wonderful memories flash back while looking at these pictures, and my thoughts come back to Bright Eyes. She forever will be the eternal light in my heart.

(Bright Eyes in the front lawn, posing for the camera)

Gunnar

(Am I the cutest dog you have ever seen? Come on, really!)

It took Mary and John a couple of months after Max died to come to the conclusion they needed another dog in their life. So come the end of August, Mary and Kevin pulled up in the driveway with a little bundle of black fur. He had that curly puppy hair and was so stinking cute. Mary was just thrilled to have a dog in the house again. She had forgotten what it was like though. Gates up, chewed-up wallpaper, pillows, and rugs. I just laughed. John would threaten every day to give the dog to me. He would say, "Max never did this." Well, you know when you have kids, and you usually have one good child and one not-so good, well, the same goes with dogs. They can't all be great. You have to throw in a little mixture now and then.

Gunnar is a great dog, just nothing like Max. He is just the opposite. If he could ruin something, he will. He was a puppy, what did you expect. When they weren't home, he would be in the foyer, but that didn't last long before he realized he could chew on the wall. It kept his interest for the time being. Then he was crated. He didn't like this, but it worked as it always does. Don't say, "ah that's mean." No, crating a dog is good for the owner and good for the dog. It keeps the dog from destroying anything in the house, so then the owner doesn't get mad, and it gives the puppy a place of his own. He's very comfortable there, and it doesn't last very long just until they are trained. Some people leave the cages up all the time. It helps when they go to a groomer or if you have to kennel your dog for some reason. They are not afraid of a cage and they go in it like it's their second home.

(Gunnar and Burbank)

Gunnar started staying with us after he was about sixteen weeks old. He loved Chelsea; Chelsea tolerated Gunnar. Being a puppy, he would jump all over Chelsea's back. She would let him for the most part then she would growl when she had had enough. Not that this would stop Gunnar at all, but it would slow him down. We would go for our morning walks and the kids on their way to school always said hi to Chelsea, and the first time we had Gunnar, he was so scared of them, he hid behind me. Then he saw that Chelsea was getting all the attention and he would slowly make his way up to the kids. From then on, you could hear Gunnar's name being yelled at all the way down the street. "Hey, look! Gunnar's back!" Then the petting would begin.

As Gunnar was getting older, he had so much spunk and energy. I would pick up Gunnar on Mondays and Thursdays and take him to Nelson's to play for the day. He would love this so much. When he was young, he had no fear, and Chip found Gunnar to be very interesting. Chip would wander off and look back to see if Gunnar was following, and almost always Gunnar would be right behind him. I could see him from anywhere I was in the house, so I would just watch him follow this Beagle around the grounds like they were on a great treasure hunt. Gunnar would come in the house just to check and make sure I was still there.

"Mary, I am having so much fun running around with Chip. He likes to explore just like me and he really seems to know the property. Is it okay if I follow him into the fields and all around? I know, I won't come back smelling bad. I promise I won't roll in anything stinky. Okay, bye. Hey, Chip. I can go but I can't go off the property so don't take me down to the lake. I don't know if I can go over the driveway to that field." He would look back as if to see if he had permission, but he didn't see me so he stopped dead in his tracks and wouldn't go past the driveway to the other fields. Chip would turn around and come back towards the house knowing Gunnar would follow. It was just as fun for Chip to have a little buddy to pal around with as it was for Gunnar.

(That's My Toy!)

Every time we would be coming down the driveway to come to Nelson's, Gunnar would be so excited he would start talking and going from side to side all excited just knowing that he was going to have a great day. I had a Camry at the time and Gunnar was doing his side to side talking. Then all of a sudden, I saw a black shadow in my side view mirror. Then in my rear view mirror, I saw Gunnar standing on the side of the driveway just watching me drive away. I gasped for air and stopped the car, got out and ran to him. I checked him all over and found nothing wrong with him. He literally jumped out of the window. He was so excited.

From that moment on, my windows were just down far enough that his head would fit out the window. It scared me at the time, but after the fact it was just hysterical. I couldn't believe how excited he would get just to be at Nelson's. That is how much he loves going there and running around. Needless to say, he never jumped out of my car again. Once again, Max would have never jumped out the window like Gunnar did. Just another difference in the two Schnauzers.

Gunnar is the light of my life. He cries when he sees me and he wants to go for a ride whenever he can. I pick him up every third Tuesday to get groomed, which he loves. He runs around in the yard first to go to the bathroom then he runs into the door and goes right in his cage until it's his time to be groomed. He looks so handsome when he is done. He loves the car ride home. On Mondays and Thursdays, I come and let him out, then we go for a car ride and back to the house. Then in the house, he runs right to the ottoman and waits for me to sit on the couch so that he can crawl up on my lap and lie there like a baby with his head lying on my shoulder while he gets his belly rubbed. So spoiled, but quite loved.

We all love when Gunnar comes and stays with us. Gunnar is so predictable. We love that about him. He is so easy. He gets along with all the dogs I have at the house, plus he loves to run around the pool with all of them. He sleeps in his bed and in the morning he gets in bed with us for a little cuddle time.. There are never any surprises with him. We hope Gunnar is around for a really long time.

(There's my little boy)

Lexi and Tyson

(Lexi)

(Tyson)

I had to do a bid on a house for a friend. I have never met David's wife Laurie, so I was excited to meet her and start cleaning for them. They have two adorable twin girls and then come to find out they have adorable twin dogs, Lexi and Tyson. Mark went with me since he was good friends with David. We were greeted at the door by both sets of twins, the girls and the dogs. The dogs look like little red foxes. They are Shiba Inu's. They are talkers. Well, Tyson more so than Lexi. Tyson loves to spend his days outside and Lexi likes to be inside and quiet and shy. They are very cute and very hairy. A lot of grooming goes into these dogs. They are very sweet and we hit it off great. I hope I get to sit them sometime soon. I clean for Laurie every other week so at least I get to see them on those days.

One day, I get this frantic call from Laurie. Lexi and Tyson were outside and they have disappeared. She had been out all morning looking for them. It was February 14 and it was the coldest winter day yet. She called all the shelters to tell them and she called the paper to put an ad in lost and found. I called all my friends that I knew lived or worked on that side of town to keep an eye out for them. When I would tell people what breed they were, they would inevitably always say, "They're what?" Then I would say they look like a red foxes. They are timid and shy with people they don't know, so it would be hard to catch them. Night was fast approaching and there was no sign of them yet. Laurie was just beside herself. It was cold and she was worried sick. No one had seen them and no calls came in that day. My biggest worry was that someone would mistake it for a real red fox and worry that it had rabies not knowing it was a dog. So I worried about someone hurting them.

Lexi came home later that day but she was alone. Laurie was so happy to see her home and safe. It was so cold that night, where in the world could Tyson be. With an ad in the paper and calls made to everyone Laurie could think of, she was worried but hopeful. Then two days later, she got a call from a lady who thought she had a fox in her backyard. Then she read the ad in her paper and realized it may be the lost dog. Tyson was sitting beside her barn and he had howled all night long. She told Laurie where she lived and Laurie drove down there right away. The lady told her husband to go make a fire in the pit so maybe the dog would come over and get warm. Laurie pulled up and she was calling for Tyson. He was a little frightened at first then he recognized her and came running. Laurie thanked the lady and was so relieved to have him home. He slept for days. She was so afraid of frost bite but he seemed to be fine, just very tired.

Mark and I went over to David and Laurie's for dinner and we were happy to see Lexi and Tyson home where they belong. At that time, we found out that Laurie thought it was so cold, so she just let the dogs out thinking they would go out and do their business and come right back in, and that's when they just took off.

I don't think they will ever do that again, but she won't ever give them the chance to even think about doing that again. A couple of months later and I couldn't resist the temptation to bust them for Laurie. I had a dog calendar with pictures of different dogs every day. Well, one of the pictures was a picture of two Shiba Inu's, so I kept the picture and got an eraser board. The next time we had a party, I put that picture up on the eraser board with the message, "If anyone finds us, please take us home. Our mother let us out and we need to get back home." At first she read it and just gave me the evil eye, then she started laughing. She asked me, "When was I going to let it go?" and I said, "Probably never." I wouldn't have said anything if it hadn't turned out the way it had, but because the dogs came home safe, I could now joke about it. I found one of those musical cards for Laurie for her birthday. It had a dog on the front and when you opened it sang, "Who let the dogs out." Then Mark and I would finish with, "Laurie did." Okay, we were done. The joke was now over and we had our fun with it. The bottom line was the dogs got home safe and it could have ended terrible but it didn't, thank God.

I see Lexi and Tyson every other Monday and I love both of them. I hope to stay with them when Laurie and David go on vacation some time so we can spend a lot more time together.

Bailey

One day, I got a call from Mary, Gunnar's mom, and she told me that her boss needed a new dog sitter. They were just not happy with the one they were using now. She said that when Bailey got dropped off at the sitter they were using now, there were at least five to nine dogs there at a time and she didn't think Bailey was very happy there. So she called me to tell me that Susie would be calling me and that she hoped that was okay with me. She also said she needed a new groomer and she thought Lisa would like to do Bailey as well, and maybe Bailey could car pool with Gunnar. I just laughed and said that was fine with me and I would look forward to hearing from her.

A few days later, I received a call and Susie would like me to meet Bailey and maybe start coming over from time to time to let him out. So when I got to the house, which was right around the corner from Gunnar's, I was pleased to see a very tiny dog. Bailey is a Japanese Chin. He only weighs about 10 pounds. He has this little face and his tongue always sticks out but goes to the left. Too stinking cute.

I was to come and let Bailey out while Susie was at work on certain days. So the first time I went there, I went right over to Bailey's couch. That's right, he has his own couch. I sat down on it because I could see that he was not too sure of me, and all of a sudden the little hairball bit me on the elbow. I just looked at him and said, "Really, was that supposed to hurt?" He just looked at me like I should be very afraid of him. Here we go another dog with "Daisy" syndrome. A tiny dog who thinks he is a German Shepherd. What is with these little toy dogs? Well, I did just what I thought would work, and like clockwork it did. I walked over to the treat cupboard and pulled one out and we became friends fast. I kept my distance as not to spook him and then we went for a walk. As time rolled on, Bailey was always so excited to see me. I got a bath of kisses whenever I came over. He loved his walks. I often laugh about our first encounter and how he bit me. Now when he sees me, he does circles, and circles, and can't wait to go with me.

I would pick Bailey up for grooming first and then Gunnar. Together we would make that long drive out. Bailey would be in the front seat and Gunnar in the back. Bailey is so tiny he couldn't see anything and he would constantly climb over to my lap so he could see out the window. I didn't blame him, however, because I thought about what he must see from down there. I tried it and all he could see was the sky. I wouldn't like that very much, not knowing where I was being driven to, so I let him crawl on my lap whenever he wanted to, just so he could see. Soon after that I bought a booster seat for Bailey for my car. Now he sits right up and can see everything. He loves his new car seat.

He loved going to Lisa's as much as Gunnar. They would both get very excited as soon as we pulled up her street. They were crying and whining as soon as we pulled into the driveway. I couldn't get the door open fast enough. They would jump out and off they would go exploring the yard, doing their business and then running down to the door to go in. When have you ever seen dogs run into the place where they get groomed? That's a great groomer.

Lisa always gets kisses right away from Bailey and Gunnar goes right into his cage. We don't even have to close the door on the crate. He just sits in it and watches us as we do Bailey's nails. I have to help with Bailey because he is just terrible when Lisa is trying to get them cut. I am not sure if something happened before at a different groomer, but he hates it. So I hold him and talk him through it every time. I always have to help, but when we are done, Lisa gets a kiss and I get kisses the whole time I am holding him. So it's not like it hurts him, he just hates getting his nails done that much. We get him done and then we move on. I leave and then I come and pick them up at 4 P.M. We do this every three weeks and they are so excited every time like it's the first.

(Chelsea sleeping and Bailey posing)

Bailey is here so often that friends are starting to believe he is ours. I think he's at my house more than he is at his home. He will follow any of our friends out to their cars and all I say is, "Bailey, you want to go?" and I put him in the car and he sits there like he's going for a ride. He doesn't care who it is, he just wants to go for that ride. Some of our friends just laugh and put him back on the ground and others drive around the block just to give the little guy a ride. So stinking cute I could just eat him up. I just snatch him up and hold him as our friends drive away, give him a kiss and set him down to walk back into our house.

You know that Bailey is a small dog, so of course he sleeps with us in the bed. He stays right down at the end of the bed by my feet. He can't jump off our bed because it's so tall, so I lift him off and on, and sometimes I find myself just carrying him around like a baby. I am not sure how old Bailey is, but I think he is four or five, so I suspect he will be around for a long time and we'll get to enjoy his company for many years to come.

(All the little ones always get along: Daisy, Bailey and BB)

Chelsea

It has been a tough year for us losing so many dogs, and as I watch Chelsea with every passing day, I know our time with her is numbered. We can barely get her to go around the block for our walks, but we do it. She wants to go, but her legs are telling her no, she'd rather stay in the yard and watch people go by.

We have a lot of parties at the house because we have the pool and that's just what happens in the summer when you have a pool. As people come, she lies there and waits to get that pat on the head. She loves the acknowledgment that she gets when people come to see her. She thinks they are here to see her and I don't tell her any different. People ask us how old she is and they are astonished that she is fifteen. I get the look from some people and I know what they are thinking. It's sad they are keeping her alive when it takes her so long to get up.

It's not time, trust me, I know. She loves being with us and she often stays up as long as we do. If she is really tired, she walks off to the bedroom often times coming right back out if we don't show up after a few minutes. Then she waddles back to the bedroom and tucks herself in.

She knows everyone in the neighborhood and gets to greet a lot of them as we go on our walk. We hear the same thing over and over, "I love Labs." We always agree with them. She greets every dog that walks by our property as if it's her duty to do so. She walks over to them all, gives them a sniff and then walks back to her lying position and life goes on. It's great to be her.

She still going for car rides with us wherever we go and still going to work with me on Mondays, Tuesdays, and Thursdays. I have to lift her into my car because she just can't hoist her legs up there. She just doesn't have the strength. We take one day at a time and love every minute we have with her. Since she goes with us to Mark's softball games, we decided to get her a ramp for the SUV so she can get in and out of the car easily. It certainly makes life easier for her.

It's June and it's warm, but she doesn't mind the heat so much. She will start to lie in the sun, but being black, she gets warm quickly, so she moves under a tree and that's just fine with her. I begin to tell Mark my concerns about her because we are going on cruise to get married and I remembered what happened the last time we went on a cruise. He shared the same concerns, but said we would cross that bridge when we came to it. I am not sure if he just didn't want to talk about it or he really meant we would deal with it as it comes. So I let the conversation go, whatever will be, will be. It's an old saying but it fits.

I look at Chelsea girl and think how lucky I was she came into our lives. And I think she probably thinks the same about us. She has had a wonderful life. The amazing thing is she's only been with us for three years, but I've known her for ten years. Three years doesn't seem like a long time, but actually it felt like a lifetime. She has touched our lives and our hearts forever.

Our cruise was coming up faster and faster. It was the beginning of July and I already had Michelle lined up to come and stay with Chelsea, and I had Lane on standby if Michelle needed any help with her. I asked Lane because she knew Chelsea and she knew what to do in case of any emergency that might come up. Michelle was grateful for that. It wouldn't matter who I asked to watch Chelsea. Anyone who knew her would have watched her, so finding someone wasn't the problem. Her health was in question at this point. You know what I say to all my clients, "You know when it's time," and now it was time for me to take my own advice. Easy to give, not easy to do.

Fourth of July and of course we are having a gathering. Chelsea is greeting everyone as she always has. She lies at our feet, and with those big brown eyes, she gets everything she begs for. Chicken, steak, and every now and then, a chip with dip if she's lucky. As you can tell from her picture, she didn't miss many meals and this day was no different. Lately, she has been putting herself to bed that she just can't stay up with us, and that was okay. She would sleep through the night barely moving. When she was out, she was out till morning. The fireworks outside never bothered her. I have a lot of dogs that bark or shake the whole time they are going off, but not her. There wasn't anything that really bothered her at all. That is what makes her the great dog she is. Easy to take care of and easy to love.

It's Sunday, a week before we are leaving on the cruise. Chelsea is out in the front yard and people are walking by and she's not even getting up to see them. She lifts her head to look at them then lies back down to sleep. I am watching her and my concerns are more warranted than ever. She's having a very hard time getting up. Her legs are just not working any more. Do I dare leave her with Michelle knowing that she may not make it through the week? Now my thoughts turn to myself.

As I watch her, I couldn't help but think, was she in pain like our friends thought when they saw her try to get up? Did I just not want to see that I was keeping her alive for me and not doing what is best for her? As I thought of what was best, my first thoughts were, it would be so easy if she would go to sleep and just keep on sleeping. And then I had my answer. I wasn't making the decision for her; I was hoping she would make the decision for me. But as I watched her struggle to get up every time she lay down, it was the answer to all my questions. I was doing this for me and me only. Mark and I talked and we decided that it was time to do what was right no matter how much it hurt.

Monday, July 16, I called the vet and told them I would be bringing Chelsea in and that I wanted to be their last client of the day. They knew Chelsea well and agreed. I took Chelsea to work with me that day. It was a sunny day. My first client was afraid of dogs, so when she saw Chelsea at her door, because she was standing there with me, she looked skeptical and I assured it would be fine. Isn't this how it always goes, Chelsea was up on her feet faster than she had been in the last three weeks, following me around and being petted by the person that didn't even like dogs. She made dog lovers out of anyone and everyone. It was time to leave my morning house as they said goodbye, they had no idea they were saying goodbye for the last time. I did, it made me cry as I drove away. It was time to go to Lane's.

I had one stop before Lane's. I had to go and talk to Ellise, not looking forward to this conversation at all. As I entered Ellise's work place, she's on the phone as usual and she gives me the hand signal to come in and sit. Pleasant as always and smiling, the conversation starts out with, "Hi, honey. How's everything going?" The tears just start to flow and I can barely talk. Of course, she is concerned because I can't even get the words out of my throat. I realized for the first time that I have finally made that decision that I didn't ever want to make. Here I was sitting in the office of Chelsea's original mom and about to tell her what I needed to tell her and I just couldn't stop crying. I finally got the words out and she just watched me in agony and I just said how sorry I was. She started to cry and came around the desk and hugged me. She told me she loved Chelsea and she loved me for loving Chelsea. She also insisted on being with me when we went.

I told her I wouldn't put her through that, and she told me she wouldn't have it any other way. I left her office and took Chelsea to Lane's.

It's a beautiful sunny day and Chelsea gets out of the car, goes in the house and right back out to lie in the sun. I called Lane and told her the story, and typical Lane, she tells me not to clean today, but to go outside and sit with Chelsea all day long. I needed to work, but often came outside to sit with Chelsea in the sun. As I walked outside, I realized she was lying next to Bright Eyes's tree. I would sit with her for a while and then go back to work. We did this all afternoon and there were several times I thought maybe I wouldn't do this today. She was walking around good and enjoying this day like she hadn't been doing for the last three weeks. Maybe she was taking a turn for the better. I called Mark and told him what I was thinking. He just said, "Mary," I said, "I know." He drove out to spend some time with Chelsea and the three of us sat together in the sun enjoying the day.

(Mark and Chelsea next to Bright Eyes's Tree)

(Me and Chelsea on one of my saddest days ever)

He knew I couldn't drive myself, so he drove us to the hospital and I called Ellise to meet us. I went in and told them that we were here, and they sent us to the back of the hospital where there was a really nice waiting area where we could spend time with Chelsea. Mark sat in the car, he just couldn't be inside with us. I understand that completely. Ellise and I were sitting on the floor with Chelsea and she got up and walked over to the door. Mark was in the car and he looked over and happened to see Chelsea standing at the door looking at him, that did him in, he just couldn't believe we were there. I saw the look on Mark's face and just called Chelsea over to sit with us. Ellise and I shared stories of all of Chelsea's antics from puppy to now, and we both had good laughs while we waited. Dr. Scott came in to talk to me and he asked me if I would feel more comfortable staying right where we were instead of moving her and we thought this would be great. Chelsea was lying on a comfortable rug surrounded by her two moms. As she lay there, I whispered to her: "Run to the Rainbow Bridge, Chelsea. Bright Eyes, Max and Burbank are waiting for you. When you see them, you stay with them and run, and play and be happy till I come to get you. You will easily recognize me. I will be the one running towards you with open arms. Her eyes closed and she sleeps. Goodbye, my forever friend."

Dr. Scott gave us both hugs and we left the hospital. The next day, Dr. Scott called me and said he knew I was very upset and he wanted to know how I was doing. I thought that was so kind. He then told me that when he tried to find a vein on Chelsea, her blood was flowing so slow and told me she most likely wouldn't have made it two more weeks. He said, "She was very frail and that we had made the right decision." Now my question was, was he telling me this to make me feel better? If so, it worked at the moment, but the pain was there for a long time.

Had we not made this decision and left on the cruise, something would have happened to her without me being there, and I would have never forgiven myself. As it is such a difficult decision to make, I can't help believe that we made the right one and that we were there for her till the end, and for this I am forever grateful.

Chelsea's ashes are buried in our garden. Over her ashes is a garden flag with that beautiful face of a black lab blowing with the wind and sitting in the sun. It's a wonderful memorial to a wonderful dog. Always remembered, always cherished.

If your dog greets you at the door with crazy enthusiasm, show him or her the same enthusiasm and their love will shine through twofold.

Pay attention to dogs. They make me smile, when I see them in a car or on a walk, or playing with other dogs, or just playing in the park, watch them and they will make you smile as well. It's good for our health and our hearts. Take them for many car rides, a lot of walks and play often with them. They don't ask for much, just our love.

To those of us that own pets, whether it be puppies or kittens, new or old dogs, saved or rescued, love them like there is no tomorrow because tomorrow comes sooner than you think, and their love is truly unconditional. Treat them with respect and honor and they will in return show you the same.

All they want is our love. Give it to them.

Acknowledgments

First and foremost, I have to thank all my clients who have shared their beloved animals with me. Without their love and generosity, I wouldn't have a story to tell. I know that these stories are just a very small part of their pets' lives and who they really are, but I want you to know that I cherish every moment that I spend with each and everyone of them. So thank you from the bottom of my heart for sharing.

Thank you to all my family and friends who have always helped me when I needed it. Thank you to my family for not caring where we are on Christmas day, but only that we are all together. Thank you, Paul, Diana and Jesse for always helping out when we needed and asked you to step in, for we know you love the animals as much as we do. Thank you, Mom and Dad for staying with Sami and Chelsea so that Mark and I could take a vacation. Thank you also for putting up with all the dogs whenever you visit. We never have a quiet house, thank you for understanding. Also, thank you from Chelsea, Daisy and Bailey for letting us all stay at your home in Virginia so we could all visit together.

Thank you to my girlfriend Michelle, for without you, Mark and I could never take a vacation or a long weekend. Our animals love you and we never worry about them when we are away. That's what makes a wonderful dog sitter. Now, I have you watching dogs at your house when I have too many at mine. I am jealous that you get to spend time with them and I don't, but I know that they are well cared for. Peace of mind is a powerful thing. Friendship is even more powerful. Thank you and I love you.

Last but not least, Mark, my husband, without your love and support I could not possibly do this job as well as I do. You are my rock. You help me with each and every dog, and to tell you the truth (though I will never admit it), the pets love you just as much as they love me. Without your time, patience, and understanding, I wouldn't be the person I am today. Without your support, I wouldn't be able to stay at someone else's house to watch their dogs while you're watching dogs at our own home. Without your foresight, I never would have thought to write a single word down. Without you, I am not me. So thank you, honey, for loving me and all of our extended family pets. We all love you.

Mary